SAINTS WHO CHANGED THINGS

By Leo Knowles

CARILLON BOOKS   *St. Paul Minnesota*

SAINTS WHO CHANGED THINGS
A CARILLON BOOK
Carillon Books edition published 1977

ISBN: 0-89310-022-6 Hardbound
0-89310-023-4 Paper

Library of Congress Catalog Card Number: 77-087154
Copyright © 1977 by Carillon Books
All rights reserved
Printed in the United States of America

CARILLON BOOKS is a division of
Catholic Digest
2115 Summit Avenue
St. Paul, Minnesota 55105
U.S.A.

CONTENTS

iii

The Difficult Apostle

Imagine yourself in the market-place at Corinth or Ephesus, around the year 50 A.D. Sunlight strikes on marble columns; a breeze wafts in from the Aegean. The market is full of chattering Greeks, Jews, Arabs and Turks—buying, selling, laughing and arguing; with, here and there, a glint of metal as a proud Roman soldier struts among them.

Suddenly a friend pulls your sleeve. "Here comes Paul of Tarsus, the Christian," he says. "Come on, I'll introduce you!"

"I'd like that," you mutter. But would you? More likely, you feel as though you had been driving along without a care in the world, and now there's a police car close behind.

If you already know St. Paul really well, then please accept my apologies. Obviously, you would not feel like that at all. But a large number of people down the centuries have had and do have this prejudice against him.

Anyone would be glad to meet Peter, or James, or John, or Matthew. They are human, just like us; especially Peter, with his obvious faults. But Paul . . . Paul is something else again. Those letters of his! Forever he is warning, scolding, cajoling—at least it seems that way.

1

Not even Peter escapes a telling-off. We can well believe that before that trip to Damascus, Paul was a very energetic persecutor.

Well, is this a fair attitude? Was Paul really so forbidding? Argument about him began during his own lifetime and continues briskly today, among learned and simple folk alike. On one thing everyone is agreed: Paul was the man who influenced the Church more profoundly than anyone apart from Our Lord Himself. So whatever we think about him, we cannot ignore him.

First, then, what did he look like? Fortunately, we have a description. If it is accurate, then those who met him for the first time must often have been surprised. For here was no large, overbearing man, but a scrawny little fellow with bandy legs, a bald head and eyebrows meeting in the middle. Only his confident stride and piercing eyes marked him as someone out of the ordinary—those and his kind, serene expression. Sometimes, it was said, he had the face of an angel . . .

For Paul, was, of course, much more than a stern school principal, sent by God to keep the unruly early Christians in order. Not only was he a highly complex character, he was also an extremely attractive one: tough yet gentle; brave yet sensitive; a Jew who fought for the rights of gentile converts; a man much loved and much loving.

Whatever lop-sided view may have come down to us, the people who actually knew Paul looked forward eagerly to his coming, hung on his every word, and wept at the thought that they might never see him again. After his death, they treasured his letters, tellings-off and all, which is why we have them today.

To understand anyone properly, we must understand his background. Paul was born, as most people know, at

Tarsus in what is now Turkey, and he never stopped being proud of the fact.

Tarsus, ten miles inland from the Mediterranean, is a prosperous commercial town even today. In Paul's time it was even more important. Standing on the main trade-route between Syria and Anatolia, it described itself modestly as "first, greatest and most beautiful."

Not only was it a commercial center, with a port and a flourishing linen industry, it was also a Roman colony whose citizens had special legal rights. So in addition to his Hebrew name, Sha'ul, the youngster also got a Roman surname, Paulus. His father may have been a leather-goods manufacturer; certainly young Sha'ul (or Saul) learned the business, for it was by making leather-goods, which probably included tents, that he supported himself later on.

Tarsus was a center of culture with a university where philosophers chopped logic all day long in elegant Greek. Paul, too, learned to speak good Greek, but he did not go to the university for his education. Instead his family sent him to Jerusalem, to study under the great Rabbi Gamaliel.

For although the family were well-to-do Roman citizens, involved in the bustling life of the city, they were also Pharisees—Jews who believed in the most rigid observance of the Mosaic Law. (In this they differed from the Saducees, whose approach was more worldly and easy-going).

From the Gospels, we get a bad impression of the Pharisees. Often, they did become the "whited sepulchres" so sternly condemned by Our Lord. It was all too easy for a Pharisee to believe that, so long as one was keeping the dietary rules, the true inner self could safely be ignored.

Yet the best of them were not hypocrites at all, but deeply sincere Jews who saw the proper observance of the Law as the necessary basis of any right relationship with God. Only by following it strictly could anyone hope to avoid sin and gain merit.

Gamaliel, Saul's teacher, was one of the very best: a wise and tolerant man who should have had a calming effect on the over-serious young student from Tarsus. Saul, for his part, respected his master and worked hard. Yet his studies brought him no peace, no inner happiness. For the more he pored over the Law, the more he felt his own inadequacy and guilt. The Law could not help to quiet his sinful desires; indeed, it seemed to make them worse. The more he knew of the Law, the easier it seemed to break it.

Paul has been called manic-depressive. Maybe he was. Clearly, at this time, he suffered from scruples and believed that any infraction of the Law, however slight, meant eternal damnation. So whenever he broke it, even by accident, he was plunged into despair.

It should surprise nobody that when the Christians appeared on the scene, Saul swore to destroy them. Fear makes fanatics; they attack what frightens them. Saul, remember, was still clinging desperately to the Law; and the more it failed him, the more desperately he clung. And now, here were these Christians, apparently suggesting that the Law was not necessary; that salvation lay with some crucified Messiah! With their weird doctrine they were hacking at his very lifeline, already so taut and frayed and close to breaking-point.

The arrest of Stephen, a fiery young Christian, on a false charge of blasphemy, must have cheered Saul up greatly. Instead of defending himself, the youngster put up a long and spirited argument for his beliefs, ending with a kamikaze attack on his judges: "You pig-headed people, you are really pagans at heart . . . you always resist the Holy Spirit just as your fathers did before you! They persecuted every single prophet who foretold the Messiah's coming, and now you have betrayed the Messiah himself—yes, and murdered him!"

Then, before they had time to recover, Stephen appeared to go into a trance. Looking up into Heaven, he informed his hearers that he could see God the Father, and Jesus standing at his right hand.

Pandemonium followed. These followers of Jesus, clearly, were both mad and dangerous! They must be destroyed, beginning with this one.

In the stoning that followed Saul played only a minor role, looking after the cloaks of the executioners. The reason could have been that by law he was too young to do any of the actual killing.

What effect the scene had upon him, we can only guess; the Acts of the Apostles says laconically that he approved of it. No doubt he did—but even Saul could not have failed to notice that Stephen, who had attacked his judges so fearlessly, died praying for them. A mad heretic, yet he could show such strength and peace, even in the face of death. How was it possible?

Soon afterwards we find the fanatical young student-rabbi going from house to house arresting Christians and throwing them into prison; soon after that, eager for more victims, he set out on the fateful journey to Damascus. When he reached his destination, as all the world knows, he was no longer a persecutor but a Christian.

Saul's conversion was a miracle, no doubt of it; Jesus spoke to him directly. Nevertheless, it was a miracle for which the Master had been preparing him. "Why are you persecuting me?" the Voice had asked. "Don't you see that it is useless to kick against the goad?" Paul had felt the goad for long enough. Now he knew whose hand it was that held it.

So Saul arrived in Damascus and, as instructed, went to the house of Judas in Strait Street. Ananias, a local Christian, had also received his instructions: he was to go to the house, find Saul, and give him back his sight. Understandably, Ananias was nervous about making a friendly approach to a man who, so far as he knew, was out to destroy the whole Christian community. Reassured, he eventually did as he was told: he restored Saul's sight and baptized him.

At last, Saul had found the peace and joy that he had sought for so long. To use his own favorite word, he was "justified." Now he knew that God loved him: had sent his Son to die for him. Ever afterwards, this was to be the centre of his teaching: the foundation of his life.

Within days, he was preaching his new-found religion in the synagogues, naturally causing a sensation. Next he moved into the country which we now call Jordan. He was there for three years, but what he did there we have never been told. Possibly he spent the time in prayer. The end of the three years found him back in Damascus where the Jews, furious at his success as a preacher, plotted to kill him. Saul, however, had got wind of the plot; while the would-be killers lay in wait for him at the gates, his friends got him out of the city in a basket.

When the Christians of Jerusalem learned that the dreaded Saul was back in town, they took cover. If news of his conversion had reached them at all, evidently they did not believe it. A kindly Jewish Cypriot convert named Barnabas came to the rescue. Saul, he assured them, was indeed a Christian now; he had done great work in Damascus. They must make him welcome.

To preach in the synagogues of Jerusalem was asking

for trouble: in Jerusalem, where he had been so well known as a persecutor. But Saul, being Saul, did just that—and in no time at all found his life threatened once more. This time he disappeared for 14 years.

About this very long period again we know next to nothing: Paul himself dismisses it in a sentence. He spent it in Syria and in Cilicia, his own home territory—apparently doing missionary work and having a thoroughly hard time in the process. Later on, he listed some of the trials which he had suffered during his travels: three shipwrecks, eight floggings, a stoning, betrayals by false brethren—some of this, at least, must have happened during the "lost" 14 years.

During this time too, he was first attacked by the "sting of the flesh" about which scholars have speculated endlessly. Most probably it was an illness of some kind—epilepsy, perhaps, or migraine; or maybe a disabling bout of depression. Since he also describes it as "an angel of Satan" sent to buffet him, it could simply have been violent sexual temptation. Whatever it was, it caused him the utmost distress, and when he prayed to be delivered from it, he was told to put his faith in the grace of God, which would be sufficient for him.

Paul believed that his affliction had been sent for a purpose; a short time before, he had enjoyed a great mystical experience, being caught up into paradise and allowed to know things which could not be put into human speech. The sting of the flesh would remind him not to give himself any of the credit: not that Paul was likely to do so, for he never got over the miracle of his own conversion. Anyhow he treated his affliction as an added reminder that all the glory belonged to God.

It was a mature apostle, then, tried and experienced, who was called to Antioch at the end of the 14 years, to work in what had become the largest of all the Christian communities. The man who fetched him was Barnabas, the friend who had smoothed his path in Jerusalem; Paul evidently regarded him as something of a father-figure and certainly as his senior in the Church. We tend to think of Paul as a comet who blazed suddenly into view and "took over" the Church's missionary activity from the moment of his conversion. In fact, it was only after a long and hard novitiate that he became the dominant figure so familiar to us all.

Antioch today is a smallish town in Syria. In Paul's time it was a large and beautiful city—third in the Roman Empire in size and importance. There was a large Jewish community with several synagogues, where the new local Church took root. Before long, converts from Jerusalem, fleeing from persecution, came to swell the ranks.

So far, the followers of Jesus had been regarded simply as another Jewish sect. Now, more and more gentiles were asking to join them. At Antioch, for the first time, they received a name of their own, Christians. At Antioch, too, they set up an altar in a cave away from the synagogue, the first Christian church. From Antioch, Paul and Barnabas set out on a mission that looked beyond the Jewish race. Three giant steps towards the future.

At first, the two missionaries made the synagogue their base jsut as they had done before. Cyprus was the first stop, Barnabas' native island. Here they had a happy and successful stay; probably Barnabas' family were influential, and that helped. At all events nobody persecuted them, and they baptized the Roman governor of the island, Sergius Paulus. Saul, of course, had the same Roman surname, and now he began to use it, perhaps at the suggestion of his distinguished convert.

When they crossed the Asia Minor (Turkey) there was a

quarrel. We do not know what caused it, but the upshot was that Mark went home to Jerusalem and Paul was extremely upset about it. Eventually he did forgive Mark but it took him a long time.

Paul and Barnabas pushed on to Antioch—not the one in Syria, which they had left, but a much smaller town of the same name perched 3,000 feet above sea-level in the province of Pisidia. True to form, they made for the synagogue and proclaimed Jesus as the Messiah. The word went round and on the following Saturday, a crowd turned up to hear them.

Some of the orthodox Jewish leaders, furious, denounced them as heretics. Paul rounded on them. "We had to preach the word of God to you first," he said. "But since you have shown yourselves unworthy of it, we'll go to the gentiles."

It was the first time this challenge had been flung down directly, and it did nothing to cool the atmosphere. So, as Jesus had directed, they shook the dust of Pisidian Antioch from their feet and moved on to Icononium, where again, after a promising start, they found themselves being run out of town.

At Lystra Paul cured a man crippled from birth; to the horror of Paul and Barnabas, the locals wanted to honor them as gods. Despite this, the Jews again drove them out; they actually stoned Paul and left him for dead. But he soon recovered and they pressed on to Derbe, where there were many converts.

Despite all their troubles, this first journey was no failure: in each town they had left a nucleus of baptized Christian believers. Under the noses of their enemies, they made a swift farewell visit to each group, then set off once more for Syrian Antioch to make their report.

Almost at once, Paul had to help settle a dispute which had rankled for some time and now threatened to split the entire Church. It came to a head when Jewish converts from Judea arrived in Antioch demanding that gentiles should be circumcised before they were baptized.

The decision, one way or the other, was going to be vital for the future of Christianity. In the first place, circumcision was, for adults, a painful and unpleasant operation; if it were to be imposed, many men would undoubtedly be deterred from entering the Church.

But much more serious, in Paul's eyes, was the implication behind the demand. What these well-meaning Jewish converts were saying, whether they realized it or not, was that the death of Jesus Christ was not enough; the Mosaic Law was still necessary for a man to be saved. To Paul, who had suffered so much anguish when he was a Pharisee, the idea was repugnant, intolerable.

The Apostles and disciples met at Jerusalem to thrash the matter out, and arrived at a sensible compromise: that gentile converts need not be circumcised but must observe some basic kosher requirements so that Jewish Christians could mingle with them without fear of ritual impurity.

That should have ended the argument, but it did not. Years later, the more stubborn of the Jewish converts were still trying to get their own way. One of Paul's angriest letters—to the Galatians—was provoked by their efforts to sabotage his ministry. And his famous quarrel with Peter, when he "withstood him to the face" was on this very same issue: for Peter was eating with gentiles when Jewish Christians were not around, and steering clear of them when Jews were present. Paul accused him of moral duplicity; in fact Peter, in his simple way, was probably just trying to be all things to all men—something that Paul himself both preached and practiced.

In 49 or 50, Paul set out on his travels once more, to revisit his converts and to spread the word still further through Asia Minor. At first he planned to go with Barnabas, but Barnabas wanted to take Mark, and Mark's earlier defection still rankled. Paul said no.

So it was with a new traveling companion, Silas, that Paul passed through Tarsus, his home town, and called at each staging-post of his earlier journey. At Lystra he took on a second companion: Timothy, son of a Jewess and a gentile father. And now Paul did a very strange thing: he circumcised young Timothy. In view of Paul's own attitude and in view of the Jerusalem decision this seems wildly inconsistent; apparently it was done to forestall Jewish hostility, which admittedly was a major hazard. Despite his stand on behalf of the gentiles, Paul himself continued to observe Jewish Law; under the Law Timothy was a Jew and Paul, who had trouble enough to contend with, was not going to give his enemies a fresh excuse to attack him.

Paul had been planning to stay in Asia Minor, but the Holy Spirit had other plans for him. At Troas, on the Aegean, he saw a vision at night—a Macedonian who pleaded: "Come over and help us."

There are good reasons for believing that the Macedonian was none other than St. Luke and that the "vision" was a flesh-and-blood visitor: the young doctor in person. At all events Luke joined the party at this stage. Together they crossed the Aegean to Greece, and the Christian Church had arrived in Europe.

One of the earliest European converts, at Phillipi, was a lady named Lydia, a purple-seller. She begged Paul and his friends to stay in her home, which they did.

It was a happy visit. Though we are often told that Paul was a misogynist, quite clearly, his women converts did not think so; and his letters, with their greetings to his special friends, show that he fully returned their affection.

Phillipi was, like Tarsus, an important local colony: the inhabitants were, like Paul, Roman citizens. He always retained a special love for the converts that he made there; they remained faithful and gave him not the slightest trouble. His letter to them is full of this love, without a word of criticism or reproach: "I thank God whenever I think of you: each time I pray for you all I pray with joy . . . you are always in my heart: God knows how I miss you all!" Once, when he was in jail, they sent him financial help and Paul remained touchingly grateful for it. It was unusual for him to accept cash from anyone, for he always prided himself on earning his keep with his own hands.

At Phillipi, too, Paul cured a poor demented girl whose masters made money out of her alleged ability as a fortune-teller. Furious, they had Paul and Silas arrested, flogged and locked up with their feet in the stocks. During the night, while they were praying, a violent earthquake lossened every prisoner's chains. The poor guard, thoroughly frightened, was about to kill himself when Paul assured him that no one had escaped. In no time at all, the man and his family had been baptized.

In the morning, the magistrates sent word that Paul and Silas were to be freed. To their consternation, Paul refused to go. "We are Roman citizens," he said, "let them come and fetch us out in person." The magistrates did come—and quickly. To ill-treat a Roman citizen could mean serious trouble. If only they had known . . .

In the end, Paul agreed to let the matter drop and to go quietly. He had taught the bullies a lesson and he had enjoyed it.

After a stay at Thessalonika, where they gave Jewish

persecutors the slip, Paul and his party arrived in Athens, where in the shadow of the Acropolis, he delivered his famous speech: "Men of Athens, I can see that you are very careful in matters of religion, for I notice among your altars one dedicated to the Unknown God. It is of this God that I have come to tell you . . ."

He got a courteous hearing until he came to the resurrection of the dead—then the jeering broke out! The great days of Greek philosophy were past; the prevailing mood was cynical. To talk to these Stoics and Epicureans about resurrection was to invite contempt. Nevertheless, not everyone jeered; some stayed to listen and, in the end, some were baptized.

Corinth next—a big city but a notorious hotbed of immorality. Nevertheless, many were baptized, including the ruler of the synagogue. This time the Jewish persecutors got no help from the Roman governor: he told them not to disturb him with their religious squabbles. Here Paul met a Christian couple who told him, to his great excitement, that there was a church already established in Rome—at the very heart of the Empire!

And so back to Antioch, but not for long. Within a few months, Paul was off again—this time to Ephesus, the great seaport on the Turkish coast of the Aegean, where, according to tradition, Our Lady spent the last years of her life.

At Ephesus, where he worked many miracles, Paul once more found himself in a head-on clash with commercial interests. The city contained the great Temple of Diana, a building two-thirds the size of St. Peter's in Rome, and the local silversmiths did a roaring trade in small models of the building, which they sold as objects of piety.

Paul's mass conversions were an obvious threat to trade; the silversmiths retaliated in a thoroughly modern

manner by staging a mass demonstration in the local theater where they yelled, for two solid hours: "Great is
Diana of the Ephesians." Paul tried to get a hearing, but
he could not. Neither could his friends; each time they
opened their mouths the crowd shouted them down.

In the end it was the town clerk who quieted them
down. The Christian visitors, he pointed out, had committed no criminal offence. If anyone wanted to bring a
civil action against them the courts were available. By
raising this tumult, they were asking for trouble: Rome
frowned on riots. He was right, and the silversmiths
knew it. Within minutes, the theater was empty. However, Paul saw that his stay at Ephesus was ended.

So he moved on to Troas, the port along the coast from
which he had first crossed into Europe. Here, one Saturday evening, he started preaching to his little band of
converts in a third-floor room which was somewhat
over-supplied with oil-lamps. Paul went on and on for
hours—in fact, until midnight. His hearers were enrap-
tured, with one exception. A lad named Eutychius, overcome by the drowsy atmosphere, nodded off and toppled
from the window where he had been sitting into the
street below.

Everyone shot downstairs. There the youngster lay,
apparently dead. As the horror took hold, and the women
began to weep, Paul came out. As always, he was calm.
Picking the boy up, he felt a heart-beat.

"Don't worry," he said, smiling. "He's still alive." And
before long, Eutychius was on his way home, not much
the worse for his fall.

Happy and relieved, everyone went inside, had a meal
and stayed talking until dawn. Paul, evidently, decided
that he had done enough preaching for one night!

Paul had now entered on the last stage of his life, and
he knew it. For he was about to return to Jerusalem,

where the danger was greatest. Famine and unrest were tearing the city apart; Christians made handy scapegoats. And yet Paul had to go. His Greek converts had given generously for their suffering brethren and the money was badly needed.

On the beach at Miletus, he met his friends from Ephesus for a heart-breaking farewell. They knelt in the sand for a final prayer, then Paul and his companions went on board. They were seeing him, he told them, for the last time.

When Paul reached Jerusalem, he was indeed put in jail just as he had forecast: though the reason for his arrest was unexpected. Some Jews from Ephesus, who were there on a pilgrimage, saw him walking the streets with a gentile Christian and falsely accused him of taking the man into a prohibited part of the Temple.

The Roman officer who arrested him was not, of course, interested in Jews' religious squabbles; but he thought that Paul looked a dangerous fellow. Possibly he was a notorious Egyptian bandit who was "wanted" at that very moment. The courage with which Paul faced a hostile mob only reinforced the impression. The officer ordered him into the garrison to be questioned under the lash, a routine method of getting the truth—or at least the desired answers—from suspects.

Paul let the soldiers tie him down before announcing, once again, that he was a Roman citizen. A Roman citizen—the magic words! Paul was hastily untied.

He was not freed, though; he remained a prisoner for the next two years, kicking his heels while a venal Roman governor waited for a bribe which was not forthcoming. During this time he survived an appearance before the Sanhedrin, whom he confounded beautifully by playing off Sadducees against Pharisees. And he survived—yet again—an attempt on his life.

A new governor, Festus, was appointed. Sure of Paul's innocence, he urged him to be tried in Jerusalem, promising him every legal safeguard. Paul, standing on his rights as a citizen, demanded to be tried before the Emperor in Rome. "If you appeal to Caesar," Festus replied wearily, "then to Caesar you must go."

Poor down-to-earth Festus! He must have been heartily glad to see the back of this brilliant Jewish crank, with his strange obesession about the Messiah. Shortly before Paul was due to leave, the Jewish King Agrippa visited Jerusalem and Paul was brought before him. Never one to miss an opportunity, Paul immediately launched into a passionate proclamation of his faith.

Agrippa was impressed. "Almost," he said drily, "you persuade me to become a Christian."

Not so Festus. "Paul, you are out of your mind," he exploded. "All that booklearning has made you mad!"

Prisoner though he was, Paul set out for Rome in a mood of keen anticipation. He had realized, years before, that if the Church was to spread throughout the world, then Rome must be its headquarters; that was why he had been so excited to learn, at Corinth, that there were already converts among Rome's Jewish colony. Straightaway he had written to them; now, at long last, he was going to meet them face to face. Of that he felt confident, for a prisoner of his standing was allowed plenty of visitors.

First, of course, Paul, his captors and the other prisoners who were traveling with him had to get there. Though none of them knew it, they were about to become involved in the most famous shipwreck in history.

If they had taken Paul's advice, they would have been spared the ordeal. By the time they reached Crete, it was obvious that they would have to stay there until spring.

No ship could sail to Italy through the winter storms. They were then in a little bay known as Fair Havens and Paul urged that they stay there, even though it did not have the facilities for a large ship. His advice was ignored: the ship put out again for Phoenice, a better harbour along the coast.

In those gales it was madness. In no time at all they were in serious trouble, unable to do anything but let the ship run before the wind. For almost a fortnight they tossed about in the open sea, completely lost, seeing neither sun nor stars. They threw the cargo overboard, and the spare tackle. It did no good. Of the 276 men on board, all but one thought that this was the end.

"Gentlemen," said Paul, "none of this would have happened if you had only listened to me. However, don't be afraid. We are not going to lose our lives, just the ship."

An angel, he said, had been sent by his God to assure him that he would reach Rome and that all his fellow-voyagers would be saved too. They would shortly be cast up on an island.

Sure enough they did, that same night, find themselves nearing land; they could not see it but the soundings left no room for doubt. The sailors, afraid of being wrecked on a rocky coast, tried to lower the boat and escape, leaving all the rest to their fate. Paul, the prisoner, realized what they were up to and warned his captors. In this crisis, he virtually took command. Even the Roman soldiers tacitly acknowledged him as their leader.

The island, of course, was Malta. The Maltese were then, as they are today, a friendly people; they built a fire on the sea-shore to warm their soaking guests. Luke, who was traveling with Paul, goes out of his way to praise their hospitality. Paul repaid it by curing their sick, including the father of Publius, the island's Roman governor. Publius became a Christian and, according to tradition, Malta's first bishop.

When spring came, prisoners and captives continued their journey in a ship called the *Castor and Pollux*. And so in the end, Paul arrived in Rome, where the Christians came joyfully out along the Appian Way to greet him.

Paul lived in Rome for the next two years, enjoying a genteel house-arrest in lodgings which he shared with his guard. Curiously, we are not told the outcome of his trial. There is some evidence that he was acquitted and that he went to Spain before returning to die a martyr's death in Rome between 62 and 64 A.D.

Perhaps the most serious charge against Paul is that he invented a religion of his own, apparently based on the teaching of Jesus but in fact alien to it.

Nothing would have wounded him more, for throughout his life Paul strove above all to preserve the integrity of Our Lord's message. Whenever he criticized or denounced fellow-Christians—which was not, after all, so very frequently—it was always because he feared that, in one way or another, they were corrupting that precious gift.

Paul invented nothing. In fact, he was not a systematic thinker but a man of frantic energy who, in a hectic and dangerous life, dealt with problems as they arose. His letters, dictated at maximum speed, often bear signs of hurried composition, though he always took care to add a few lines at the end in his own hand.

Yet despite the pressures under which he worked, and despite his volatile temperament, Paul's was a profound and penetrating mind. Those years spent poring over the Law were not wasted. He saw, as simple fishermen sometimes could not, the implications of what Jesus taught. It is not surprising to find Peter remarking rue-fully that Paul is sometimes hard to understand.

Paul sees clearly, for example, what baptism really means: to be baptized is to become a child of God. If we are children of God, then the divisions which keep men apart—Jew and Greek, slave and free—can no longer have any meaning for us.

We live in a world very different from Paul's but still we need his help. For we, too, must apply the Gospel to the problems of our time, and it is Paul, the Church's first and greatest thinker, who will help us to find the right questions and the right answers.

The Man Who Built
On Sand

One day around the year 270, a young Egyptian named Antony went to church and heard a sermon which hit home as nothing ever had before. It was about the rich young man who wanted to be perfect and the advice Our Lord gave him: sell all you have and give to the poor.

Antony had recently become a rich young man; his parents had died leaving him a 200-acre farm. Unlike the youngster in the Gospel, he decided to obey the advice. He sold the farm, gave the proceeds away, and asked some good women he knew to look after his young sister. Then he set about the job of becoming perfect.

At this time he was 20 years old. He had not had much schooling, if any. At school the boys were rough; Antony was gentle and sensitive, so his parents did not send him.

Nevertheless, he trained himself for his new life in a thoroughly systematic way. He went around visiting with all the really holy men he knew—men who had devoted themselves to prayer and self-denial. He watched how they prayed, what they ate, observed when they got up and when they went to bed. Above all, he talked to them about the spiritual life. When they taught him all they could—and it took many years—Antony went to live among some old rock-tombs outside Koman, his home village. He was seeking a solitary life, but it was not solitary enough. So, at the age of 35, Antony headed for the desert.

He soon found just the spot he needed, in a ruined fort on a mountain east of the Nile. There he would spend the rest of his life in total solitude. The rest of the time would be spent in prayer and meditation. A kind friend was ready to provide the little bread he needed to keep him alive.

Antony was not the first man to choose the desert as the ideal place for being alone with God. Elijah had done the same long before Our Lord's time. So had John the Baptist. So had the Essenes—the Jewish sect who left us the Dead Sea Scrolls. So, probably, had other devout Egyptians—men like those with whom Antony had studied. Antony had no reason to expect that things would not work out just as he had planned.

But they did not. For 20 years, he fought a losing battle against the people who, as news of his wisdom and holiness got around, began to call on him in ever-increasing numbers. At first he shouted advice from behind his rock barricade, but in the end, they broke it down and made him come out. Some wanted counseling, others simply wanted him to pray for them. Some were men who themselves wanted to be hermits and who thought, rightly, that Antony was the best man to teach them.

When he had taught them, however, they did not, as he expected, go off and find a patch of desert where they too could be alone. They stayed right there around the mountain, building their little thatched cells only a few yards away, first one, then two, then half a dozen; until one morning Antony woke up, looked out and realised that he had founded a Community.

It was the very last thing he had intended to do, and a

lesser man might have been dismayed. Antony shrugged his shoulders. If this was God's will, there was nothing more to be said. To refuse these men his help and guidance would be unthinkable.

So Antony became the first abbot of the first monastery. Of course, it was nothing like the sort of monastery we know, for Antony was no organizer. The hermits in their huts, now scattered in growing numbers across the desert, followed no settled rule, did no work together, and at first did not even meet regularly for prayers.

Instead, each brother spent most of his time inside the cell, occupied with his own prayers and with weaving mats and baskets from rushes. The main object of this work was to ward off idleness, though sometimes the products were sold to raise a little money for bread. There might, also, be a little patch of garden in front of the cell, in which wheat and vegetables were grown.

Vegetables, though, were very definitely a luxury. Antony and his monks lived mostly on bread, flavoured with rock-salt, and a little water—one meal a day, taken at sunset. The bread was of a kind that most of us have never tasted and, hopefully, never will. It looked and felt like small rocks. It was baked only once or twice a year and it had to be soaked in water before it could be eaten. The monks' ordinary dress was a rough sheepskin.

Though he had left the world behind, the desert monk enjoyed no sheltered, peaceful existence. Some of the most terrible battles in human experience were fought out there among the sands and boulders of Scete and Wadi Natrun.

For there, in the desert, Satan was a constant and ever-present menace: tangible, visible, as real as the snakes and scorpions that slithered among the rocks.

I do not mean, by this, simply that the brothers suffered violent temptations, though many of them did. I

mean that the monks—Antony above all—were attacked
by the powers of Hell, quite literally; attacked in violent
and dreadful ways.

In every age, including our own, a few unfortunate
people have been subjected to these demonic attacks.
The Curé of Ars was one well-known victim; other cases
are equally well-attested.

The demons, of course, never took possession of Antony, but they tried practically everything else. Antony,
wise to every satanic trick, seemed at times almost to
enjoy the running battle that he fought.

First, they tried conventional methods of temptation.
They tried to make him think of the money he had given
away, the power and fame he might be enjoying, and of
the dearly loved sister whom he had left behind when he
came to the desert. Sanctity, they urged, was a loser's
game: hard, dreary and unrewarding.

Next. Satan himself appeared to Antony as a woman
and tried seduction. (The monks, incidentally, believed
that their enemy had got a daughter—perhaps because
he so often used this method of approach!)

All ordinary temptations having failed, he turned up
next in the guise of a little boy, though apparently making no attempt to conceal his identity. "Oh, Antony, you
are so strong," he crooned. "You're the only man in the
whole world whom I can't persuade to commit sin." But
Antony was not falling for that one either.

On the following night, Satan burst into Antony's cell
and beat him so violently that his friends, finding him
bleeding and unconscious, at first thought that he was
dead. They were actually mourning, gathered round his
body, when he showed signs of life and began to recover.

The third night Satan was back again, this time with a
noise like an earthquake. First he appeared as a roaring
lion, which rushed at Antony and seemed about to de-

vour him. The lion became a bull, huge and angry, thundering towards him with horns lowered. The bull disappeared and there was a serpent, writhing and sinister, its poisonous fangs forking from its huge mouth. Suddenly the serpent was gone, and in its place a ravening wolf, with jaws gaping for the saint.

The wolf vanished, and there stood Jesus, come at last to rescue the exhausted Antony.

"Lord, why didn't you come before?" Antony demanded. Saints are never afraid to speak their minds.

"I was right behind you all the time, Antony," said Jesus. "I just wanted to see how well you held out." And He promised him that because he had fought so well, his influence for good would grow and endure.

Moving and dramatic though these stories are, they are not the most valuable legacy that Antony has left us. Few of us, fortunately, are likely to suffer such ordeals.

But the battles which Antony and his monks had to fight against themselves bring them much closer to us. Out there in the wilderness they learned a great deal about the human soul and the difficulties that face anyone who tries to put God first. For the desert was nothing more nor less than a vast laboratory of the spiritual life; happily, its findings have been made available to us all.

Take, for example, that commonest of bugbears, discouragement, weariness—what saints of a later age called *accidie*. With all his great holiness, Antony did not escape this; we know that he suffered a bad attack on at least one occasion. Quite suddenly, he got the feeling that all his efforts were useless, he was wasting his time in the desert, and could not concentrate on his prayers.

After praying to be delivered from the mood, he went outside and saw, to his surprise, a man he did not know plaiting palm leaves. The man stopped, began to pray, and after a while continued to work. Soon, there was another pause for prayer, then the man turned. "Do as I am doing, and you'll get through your trouble," he said. Then he disappeared. The moral is so obvious that Antony did not even bother to state it.

Pharisaism, also, constantly had to be fought. On one occasion, a monk who had sinned was solemnly ordered from the church in front of everyone. A holy old monk called Bessarion got up and went out with him. "I'm a sinner as well," he said simply.

Another monk, a bishop called Ammon, was asked to lead a raid on the cell of a monk suspected of harboring a woman. Ammon happened to know that the woman was hiding in a water-jar, and when the search-party arrived, he sat on it. Finding nothing amiss, the searchers eventually left, Ammon going out last. At the door, he turned. "Watch your soul," he said simply.

Some monks, on the other hand, went to lengths that we would consider unhealthy. One of these, seeing a group of nuns approaching, turned aside lest he suffer from exposure to their female presence. The Mother Superior, evidently an early feminist, eyed him stonily. "If you had been a perfect monk," she said, "you wouldn't even have noticed that we were women."

Hard as the monks were on themselves, they were ready to break the rules in the name of charity. Visiting a brother who was sick, Antony's assistant Macarius asked him if there was anything he would like.

"Some honey-cakes, please," replied the sick one.

Honey-cakes were an unheard-of luxury, but Macarius did not bat an eyelid. Instead he walked 60 miles to get them.

Another favorite story is that of two old hermits who had lived together in perfect amity for many years. One day, the senior of them proposed that, just for the heck of it, they should try to have a quarrel.

"But I don't know how to," said his companion.

The first monk picked up a stone and put it on the ground between them.

"Now," he said. "You pretend that this is your stone, and I'll deny it and say it's mine, and that way we'll start to quarrel.

Obediently, his companion declared: "That's my stone."

"No, it isn't, it's mine," said the other.

"All right. If it's yours, you take it," came the reply.

Never before and never afterwards was there anything in history quite like this mass flight to the desert. Within a very few years, not merely hundreds but thousands of men—and women too—had left their often comfortable homes to live that life of incredible austerity. In their search for God many, like Antony, became saints.

Soon vast tracts of sand and mountain were covered with cells: whole towns were given over to them. Day and night the prayers rose to Heaven—not the popular devotions of our time, of course, but psalms and other passages from Scripture; for then, as now, the Bible was the basis of all monastic prayer. Some monks, it was said, could recite the whole of the Old and the New Testaments by heart.

A crowded desert is a contradiction in terms, but that is what happened. Moreover, for hermits seeking solitude, visitors were a continuing problem. Not all came seeking help: some were simply sightseers, out to satisfy their curiosity. For the monks, like the Sphinx and the Pyramids, had become a tourist attraction.

Often the more determined solitaries removed themselves to swamplands and other unattractive spots, in the hope that there they would be left alone. Yet still their would-be admirers pursued them.

One hermit, with a great reputation for sanctity,

scrambled into a palm tree when, one day, he spied unwelcome visitors on the horizon. Since it was the only palm tree for miles around, he knew that he would certainly be spotted.

"Who are you looking for?" he demanded as the intruders approached, knowing perfectly well what the answer would be.

When they told him, he said: "Oh, you don't want to waste your time on him. He's crazy."

The visitors, who had already come to that conclusion about their informant, went on their way thoroughly bewildered.

By this time Antony himself had gone off in search of more solitude. After 20 years on his mountain at Pistris, he decided to remove himself to a place called Thebaid, where the desert looked more promising. However, a voice from Heaven came up with a more practical suggestion.

"You'll have twice as much trouble at Thebaid," it said. "Better try the Inner Desert instead."

So Antony, guided by some local Arabs, crossed the Nile and, after a three-day march, came to a beautiful spot where a mountain, higher and lonelier than the one he had left, looked out across the Gulf of Aqaba close to the Red Sea. It looked across to Mount Sinai, where God gave the Ten Commandments to Moses. At the base of the mountain was a spring of clear water and a few date-palms—all that he needed. Antony fell in love with the place at once, and spent the rest of his life there.

Antony and his monks have been called basically selfish because they ran away from the world to concentrate on saving their own souls, a charge which is sometimes leveled at contemplative monks and nuns even today. It was, and is, an unfair accusation, and especially so in Antony's case.

For even in his new home, Antony was sought out by people who needed him. Once again he never refused to help, whether the supplicant was a poor peasant or somebody important and influential, like the judges who, in difficult cases, marched their prisoners in chains before him to beg his counsel in reaching a just decision.

Once, when Antony was in town, a military commander begged him to stay longer. The request produced one of the saint's most quoted replies: "Fish, if they try to stay on dry land, quickly die. It's the same with us monks. If we stay away from our cell for long, we soon forget our true vocation."

And what, you may wonder, was he doing in town? Hermit though he was, Antony kept in constant touch with the troubles of his fellow-Christians in Alexandria, and on two occasions he led a group of monks out of the desert to help them. Throughout Antony's life, Egypt was plagued by unrest, famine and oppression, for the country was under Roman occupation.

The Emperor Diocletian had barred Christianity as a threat to the official religion, and although he was now dead, sporadic persecutions continued in the East for years afterwards. In the year 311 Egypt's Roman governor, Maximin Daja, launched yet another attack on the local Church.

Antony, hearing the news, joyfully made for Alexandria in the hope of achieving martyrdom. As soon as they arrived, he and his monks marched to the court-room and called out encouragement to the Christian prisoners as they were led in.

They were expecting the judges to order them arrested. In fact, they were simply ordered off the premises. But when the court next sat, there were Antony and friends in their accustomed places. Strangely, they were not molested: possibly the Romans thought that they

were mad. Denied their martyrs' crown, Antony and his
companions went round the jails where the prisoners
were held, and the mines where they were put to slave
labor, and brought them new comfort in their ordeal.

Antony's second expedition to the big city, years later,
was made in a very different mood. Now the Church had
a new cross to bear, for the Arian heresy had swept
through Egypt and threatened to split the Christian
community in two.

Arius, a devout but misguided pastor in one of Alexandria's parishes, stared to teach a view of Christ which
meant, in effect that He was not God—that He was a sort
of second-class god. (More about this in the next chapter).

Arius's ideas swept through the Church like wildfire;
the row became bitter and there was violence on both
sides. Antony's prestige was great. If the Arians could
get him on their side, they would gain even more ground.
So, unscrupulously, they put it about that Antony had
been heard to give public support to their views.

Antony, when he learned about it, was outraged. In no
time at all he was on the road to Alexandria, a few trusted
friends behind him, all set to give the Arians a piece of
his mind.

He must have been a strange spectacle, as he stood
there in the market-place, denouncing the heretics and
all they stood for. Dressed in his rough sheepskin, his
hair and beard long and matted with filth, his body covered with the grime of half a century, Antony looked
more like the Wild Man from Borneo than a Christian
saint. Nevertheless, he inspired only reverence in his
orthodox beholders.

The modern Christian—at least in the West—believes
that cleanliness is next to godliness. Antony and his followers believed the exact opposite. He had now been a

monk for more than 50 years and in all that time he had
never washed himself, never combed his hair, never
even put his feet in water except when fording a stream.
Washing and bathing, like meat and wine and fine
clothes, were regarded as worldly luxuries and definitely
not for monks.

If that sounds incredible, remember that Antony was
comparatively moderate: he did not believe in overdoing
the self-denial. "Some monks have destroyed their own
health with too much abstinence," he observed gravely.
"They lack prudence, and so they are still far from God."
He did not go along with those whose motto was: "Eat
grass, wear grass, sleep on grass."

For now other leaders were arising in the desert, men
who reverenced Antony but had ideas of their own. Of
these the greatest was Pachomius, an ex-soldier and a
convert from paganism, who brought his military mind to
bear on the monastic life and began to organise the kind
of religious Community which we have today.

Had Pachomius stayed in the army, he would have
been an outstanding general. He founded not one
monastery but several, each under its own head.
Nevertheless he remained in overall charge.

Monks, he insisted, must work for their living, and so
each monastery was given a different trade. At the house
of weavers, the house of potters, or the house of bakers, a
monk produced goods for sale in the town, combining
regular labor with regular prayer in the mode later
adopted by St. Benedict. Like a Benedictine house,
Pachomius' monasteries had dormitories, a refectory, a
library, a garden and workrooms, in a pattern which remains basically the same today.

Of course, General Pachomius put his men into
uniform—the first religious habit. It was he who invented
the cowl which monks have worn ever since.

Curiously, Antony and Pachomius never met and this Antony regretted, for he thoroughly approved of Pachomius's reforms. Clearly organization was needed, now that monasticism had become a mass movement, and he welcomed a man with the genius to make it a fact.

Although, in the centuries to come, there would always be some religious men who preferred the solitary life, it was the organized Community which was to set the pattern for most.

Though some desert monks were priests and some, even, were bishops, most remained in the lay state. Neither Antony nor Pachomius was ever ordained.

Despite the apparent harshness of early monastic life, or perhaps because of it, the brothers frequently lived to a great age. When Antony died he was 105. Since he had a horror of being mummified, he made the brothers promise never to tell where he was buried. His only possessions, a couple of sheepskins, he left to two friends.

Though Antony has no tombstone, he has got a memorial, for there is, to this day, a monastery on his beloved mountain at Pismir. It is one of several which still flourish in the desert.

Every year, young Egyptian Christians leave comfortable homes, just as Antony did, to seek a life of prayer in these desert monasteries. Lawyers, factory-workers, students and businessmen, they live much as those first hermits did 17 centuries ago. Those who have visited them agree on one thing: that despite the physical hardships, nowhere are there happier or more cheerful men. Antony would be pleased, but not surprised, to hear them say so.

Trouble With
The Trinity

Among the thousands of young men who followed Antony into the desert was a youngster from Alexandria named Athanasius. We know little about his background save that his parents were Christians and that he had been a brilliant pupil at school.

It is not even clear whether he went to the desert with the intention of becoming a monk and if so, why he did not stay. Anyhow, he did not, although he and Antony remained lifelong friends. By the year 325 young Athanasius was one of the secular clergy of Alexandria; not a priest but a deacon, yet doing an important job as assistant to Bishop Alexander.

There have been fewer more important years in Christian history than 325. For on May 25th, at Nicaea in Northern Turkey, bishops from all over the known world gathered to decide once and for all what the Church really believed about the Second Person of the Blessed Trinity. Was He, as we believe, one in substance with the Father, proceeding from Him from all Eternity? Or did the Father create Him from nothing at some point in time?

If you read the last chapter you will recognize the second proposition as the one taught by Arius, the

Libyan-born priest whose followers provoked Antony to leave the desert and come into Alexandria to denounce them. If Arius was right, then Jesus could not really be God. At best, He would be a demi-god.

The Arian heresy belongs to the history-books now; yet in its day it far exceeded in force and violence any of the issues which divide Catholics at present.

To understand its impact—and to understand Athanasius—we have to recapture the atmosphere which early Eastern Christians lived and breathed. To us, a dispute about the doctrine of the Trinity would be strictly for theologians—certainly not a topic that hairdressers and stockbrokers would argue about in restaurants. In 4th-century Egypt, Syria and Palestine, it was a very different story.

"If you go into a shop in the Eastern Empire," said St. Gregory of Nyssa, "the cashier will start talking about the Begotten and the Unbegotten instead of giving you your change. The baker, instead of telling you how much his loaves cost, argues that the Father is greater than the Son. And if you want a bath, the attendant assures you that the Son most certainly proceeds from nothing."

When Arius composed a song to promote his view of the Trinity, two laymen called Flavian and Diodorus marched into church with a crowd of friends chanting "Glory be to the Father *and* to the Son, *and* to the Holy Ghost," to drown the heretical chorus.

In the West, law and discipline were more important than theological speculation. But in the East, dogma was all: it ruled the whole life, politics included. Careers stood or fell by the presence of a single letter in a Greek word: *homoousios*, of the same substance; *homoiousios*, of like substance. About this issue, lifelong friends might come to blows and never speak to each other again. Sometimes there were riots and people were killed.

It was because the quarrel had become so bitter and so widespread that Constantine, the Roman Emperor, summoned the Council of Nicaea to settle the matter once and for all. The Church, he declared, should be a force for unity: its quarrels were a disgrace. With two exceptions, the bishops voted for the orthodox definition, and so gave us the Creed which we still recite at Mass.

And there, you might expect, the argument ended. In fact, it had barely begun. For many of the bishops at Nicaea were in fact Arians at heart, while others held views which tended towards Arianism. They were only biding their time.

Why had they voted against their own beliefs, these bishops? Quite simply, because Constantine in person had presided at the Council, and he sided with the orthodox opinion. Had the Arians got to him first, he might just as easily have sided with them, for he considered the whole argument a mere quibble over words. As it was, few were willing to cross the Emperor, even though he had proclaimed a policy of religious toleration. Persecution was still too fresh in most minds.

When, three years later, Alexander died and Athanasius became bishop, he had no illusions about the Arians. He had been at Nicaea and he knew that, sooner or later, they would attempt a come-back. Although, as a deacon, he had played little actual part in the Council, he himself had always been a passionate upholder of the orthodox position.

For the time being, the Arians continued their strategy of apparent submission. Arius himself, at a personal interview with Constantine, signed a declaration which seemed near enough to orthodoxy to satisfy the Emperor's untheological mind. Constantine, more concerned with peace and order than with doctrinal definitions, ordered that all excommunicated Arians be reconciled to the Church. Athanasius, who did not trust them, refused.

For the Arians and their allies, Nicaea had been a huge set-back. By persuading Constantine to lift his ban on them, they had regained valuable ground. Now here was Athanasius, a young upstart of barely 30, standing in their path. He must be crushed!

They dared not attack his orthodoxy, so they attacked his character instead. First, they accused him of destroying an altar and upsetting a chalice, because he 'disapproved of the priest's doctrinal views. A commission went to visit the spot, and found that no church existed there. The Arians, incensed, relieved their feelings by getting Jews and pagans to attack the local Christians.

The next accusation was more serious: Athanasius had killed a bishop named Arsenius and dismembered his body for use in black-magic rites. Arsenius was produced alive and in one piece.

All the same, said the Arians, Athanasius *was* a sorcerer. He, had interfered with the trade-winds and delayed the grain-boats on which Egypt depended. But by this time, Athanasius, weary of the whole pantomime, had gone off to Constantinople to ask the Emperor for a personal hearing in the presence of his accusers.

Constantine himself recorded his surprise when the tiny bishop—a later Emperor called him a "mannikin"— suddenly jumped from the roadside and placed himself in the path of the imperial horse. Having listened to his plea, Constantine decided that it was reasonable and appointed a date for the hearing.

Then suddenly, unaccountably, he changed his mind. Athanasius, he declared, would be banished—to Trier, now in West Germany but then the capital of Belgian Gaul.

What produced this peculiar about-face? Possibly

Constantine believed that Athanasius really had been tampering with the winds; more likely, he held him responsible for causing the whole dispute. After all, if Athanasius had reconciled the Arians as instructed, peace would have reigned.

Distressed and bewildered, Athanasius must have felt like a hijacked air traveler. Instead of returning, as he had expected, to his sunny diocese, here he was, through no fault of his own, dumped down among barbarians in the mist and cold of Northern Europe!

Fortunately the exile did not last, for Constantine died in the very next year. To make sure of Heaven, he had purposely delayed Baptism until the end of his life. The bishop who baptized him was one Eusebius of Nicomedia, an Arian and the leader of the campaign against Athanasius.

So the stalwart little bishop found himself back in Alexandria, but not for long. His enemies renewed their attacks, all the old charges were revived, Athanasius was deposed and a warrant issued for his arrest. When he fled to the harbor he found that all ships had been forbidden to leave. Somehow he persuaded a captain bound for Italy to smuggle him on board, and the ship slipped out under cover of night.

Once in Rome, he appealed to Pope Julius. The Pope, after a full investigation, dismissed all charges against him and ordered him reinstated. But there was no going back to Alexandria, at least not yet.

For in his absence a notorious Arian called Gregory had been installed as bishop. This man, described as "a monster from Cappadocia", employed what was now becoming a familiar Arian tactic. He recruited a mob of pagans, Jews and town roughnecks to beat up the orthodox Catholics and desecrate their churches. Women were raped, monks attacked, funds stolen. Pagan offerings of birds and pine-cones were placed on Catholic altars and church candles burned before idols. One church was set on fire. Squads of police rounded up Catholics of known orthodox views.

When the Pope's order to reinstate Athanasius arrived, the Arians and their allies responded by calling a council of their own at Antioch. True to form, they produced three creeds in rapid succession, different in dogma, united in condemning Athanasius.

We can imagine how the tough little man must have felt—not for himself, but for his flock who were suffering so much. And there was he in Rome, powerless to help!

Once again, however, the tide turned suddenly in his favor. At his death, Emperor Constantine had been succeeded by his three sons. They were called, somewhat confusingly, Constantine II, Constans and Constantius. Some of their more patriotic subjects compared them to the Blessed Trinity. Their first action, on gaining power, had been to massacre all their male relatives with the exception of two babies.

Predictably, the trio did not stay united for long, and soon Constantine Junior fell in battle against the troops of brother Constans. That left Constans as sole ruler in the West, while Constantius reigned in the East.

In Constans, Athanasius found an unexpected friend. He appealed to Constantius to allow this brave Egyptian to return to his diocese and Constantius agreed. Indeed, he could do little else. For in the end the violence of the Arians had reacted against them and sickened even some of their former supporters. Gregory, the usurper, was assassinated. The people of Alexandria wanted their bishop back.

Never in the long history of the city was there a day quite like that day in 346 when, once again, Athanasius stepped off the boat which had brought him from exile and walked through the streets to his home. Crowds cheered and wept; torchlight processions kept the excitement going far into the night. Long afterwards, when people wanted to describe a wonderful time they would say:"It was like the day when our Bishop came home."

Athanasius, in fact, had not shown himself over-eager. Much as he wanted to return, he had learned not to put his trust in princes. So, before finally accepting Constantius's invitation, he had been careful to get it in writing. As an added precaution, he visited the Emperor and received his personal assurance that no further false accusations would be believed.

The next ten years were years of comparative peace. The bishop of Egypt rallied to the support of Athanasius and so did the desert monks, many of whom he appointed to dependent sees. At last the bishop could get on with a bishop's business: running the diocese, looking after his flock, building up the Church.

One day, a visitor showed up at the palace with a remarkable story. His name, he said, was Frumentius and he was a native of Tyre, the Phoenician seaport which is now in Lebanon. When they were children, he and his brother had been taken by their uncle on a voyage to Ethiopia.

On the return journey, barbarian pirates had murdered their uncle and the ships' crew, and the two youngsters, both Christians, had been sold as slaves to the King of Ethiopia. They had become his favorites, Frumentius especially. When he grew up, he was appointed tutor to the royal children and, when the king died, Regent of the whole nation.

His position had helped him to convert many of the Ethiopians to Christianity, and now they needed a bishop. Could Bishop Athanasius please help?

Athanasius, greatly impressed, consulted several of his

colleagues. They interviewed Frumentius and agreed: no better bishop could be found than the missionary himself. So Frumentius, no doubt to his surprise, was swiftly consecrated and sent back to continue the good work. (Even today, though the Ethiopian Church has recently become independent, its Patriarch is still consecrated by the Coptic Patriarch of Alexandria).

In 350, Athanasius's friend Constans was murdered by a rebel named Magnentius. This left Constantius, the sole survivor of the original trio, as ruler of the entire Empire. Once Constantius had defeated his brother's killer, which he quickly did, his power was complete.

Athanasius must have guessed it: this could only mean trouble. For Constantius, a bandy-legged dwarf who affected a booming voice, fancied himself a theologian, and his views were far from orthodox. Insofar as they could be classified at all, they were distinctly Arian.

His first move was to accuse Athanasius of conspiring with his brother's murderer, a charge which Athanasius easily refuted. Then he tried to trick him into leaving the diocese temporarily—obviously with the object of preventing his return. Athanasius did not fall for this, either.

Though in some ways a stupid man—his intellectual pretensions were ridiculous—Constantius was also cruel, ruthless and determined. Also, he had luck on his side, for Pope Julius had died and Liberius, a much weaker man, had been elected in his stead.

At Arles, in France, Constantius called a council and packed it with Arian bishops. Liberius sent two delegates, whose job was to stand up for Athanasius. Unfortunately, they proved to have no more courage than their master, for they allowed themselves to be bullied into doing exactly the opposite. They signed a declaration condemning him.

Liberius, very angry, demanded a full council. Constantius agreed; it was just what he wanted. He was confident that he could swing it against Athanasius and remove him once and for all.

The council took place in the principal church of Milan in the year 355. The bishops met in the sanctuary, behind a curtain. The people of the city gathered in the nave.

Soon episcopal voices were raised. The laity quickly guessed what was happening: the Arian bullies were at their work. "Down with the Arians," they yelled. "We want none of that heresy here!"

The Catholic bishops, no doubt encouraged by this display of support, refused to be browbeaten. Furious, Constantius called them to his palace and gave them an ultimatum: sign, or be banished along with Athanasius.

Still the bishops stuck to their guns. "We can't condemn anyone without a hearing," they told him. "It's against Canon Law."

"Don't talk to me about Canon Law," boomed Constantius. "My will is Canon Law!"

The threat was carried out; the loyal prelates were banished. The people of Milan got an Arian bishop for their pains.

So once again, Athanasius found himself deposed—but this time he dug his heels in. He refused to be banished. Constantius tried threats and he tried persuasion. Neither had any effect. Anthanasius would not leave Alexandria. He had, he pointed out, been recalled to the city by Constantius himself. Furthermore, he had the Emperor's sworn promise that he would be allowed to remain there undisturbed, that there would be no more false accusations.

Only one thing was left to the Emperor—force. As Athanasius celebrated Mass in Alexandria's Church of

St. Theonas, 5,000 Roman troops surrounded the building.

Informed of their presence, Athanasius seated himself
on the bishop's throne and gave out the 136th Psalm, a
mighty expression of confidence in God through which
runs a continuing refrain: "For his mercy lasts for ever."
This line the congregation recited. They were still recit-
ing it when the soldiers burst in.

They did not get Athanasius. How he escaped he
never knew; he collapsed and his flock smuggled him
out unconscious. While a house-to-house search went on
through the length and breadth of Alexandria, the
wanted man was out of the city and away into the desert,
to his friends the monks.

Athanasius was now 60, an age at which most men
want to take life a little more quietly. Yet his next six years
were spent on the run, constantly moving from cell to
cell in monk's disguise, slipping up and down the Nile
by boat at night; always one jump ahead of the soldiers.
St. Antony was dead now but the men he had left behind
were more than ready to take a risk for Antony's friend.
And, unworldly though they were, they were cunning
enough to outwit the pursuers every time.

Once, when things got really hot, Athanasius hid out in
an old cistern. Then he moved to the home of a young
woman who was so beautiful that no one would ever
have thought of looking for him there. She fed him and
also kept him supplied with paper and ink; for whatever
the difficulties or dangers, Athanasius always found time
for writing.

According to one story, he even turned up in disguise
at one of the councils which Constantius continued to
organize. It probably is just a story. All the same, it
would have been entirely in character.

For all his boldness, though, Athanasius could do nothing to help his own people—for once again, the Arians
had taken over in Alexandria. The new usurper was one
George, a dishonest pork butcher turned bishop. Like
Gregory before him, he set up a reign of terror among
the city's loyal Catholics.

But they were not alone in their trouble, for now Con-
stantius tried to make a heretic of the Pope himself.
When poor Liberius refused to sign, he was exiled to
Thrace, a remote region between the Danube and the
Aegean. There he languished for two years, while on the
papal throne sat Felix, a puppet of the Emperor.

The Emperor visited Rome in person—and, just as in
Milan, the laity stood up bravely for the truth. "One God,
one Christ, one Bishop!" they shouted. Constantius
heard and took notice.

They could have Liberius back, he told them, if he
would sign a new creed; one that was broadly worded
and should not trouble his conscience. The document
was taken to Liberius in Thrace. "Sign or die," he was
told. The Pope signed.

We do not know what was in the creed, for no copy of it
has survived. Probably, it was vague rather then heretical. Liberius was allowed to return to Rome, and Constantius turned his attention to a Spanish bishop who,
like Athanasius, had always spoken out boldly for orthodoxy. Hosius of Cordova was over 100 years old, but it
did not save him from torture. He was put on the rack
and his bones stretched until he signed the Emperor's
creed.

In his desert hiding-place, Athanasius heard of the de-
fections. He refused to blame either Hosius or the Pope.
Only the Emperor he condemned, and he condemned
him bitterly.

Few would deny it, even today: this was the worst

time in the whole history of the Church. Every fully Catholic bishop had been removed from his diocese; the Pope himself had been forced into what looked like a compromise with heresy, and even so he had to share his throne with the antipope Felix.

But the gates of hell did not prevail. In fact, they crumpled and collapsed fairly quickly. For by now the bishops whom I have been loosely calling Arian were no longer, for the most part, Arians in the strict sense. They represented a whole range of opinion, varying from near-Arianism to near-orthodoxy, and they bickered endlessly among themselves. In order to get final agreement, Constantius had to bully them into signing yet another compromise creed, this time one which merely condemned "all who say the Son is a created being like other created beings." Since nobody *had* said that, its effect was nil. "The Church trembled and groaned to find itself Arian," wrote cheerful old St. Jerome—a memorable sentence, but happily not true.

The bishops, in fact, were thoroughly fed up. For years they had been ordered about all over the Empire, attending endless councils, spending long periods away from home, and making themselves look ridiculous in the process. There had even been times when the mail could not get through because the roads were clogged with bishops hurrying to yet another council. And what had been the end of it all? A meaningless compromise!

Even before the final debacle, some of them had been heard to mutter: "Hadn't we better get back to the faith of our fathers? Are we supposed to go on drawing up creeds for ever?"

When Constantius finally died, in 361, even he was weary of the bickering and the hair-splitting.

For the third time, Athanasius returned to Alexandria, to a welcome hardly less enthusiastic than the previous one. Like Gregory before him, George, the butcher-bishop, had come to a sticky end. Outraged by his cruelty, the Alexandrians had torn him to pieces.

The new Emperor, Julian, had been a Christian but was now once more a pagan—Julian the Apostate. Like Constantine, he wanted tolerance; but he wanted unity above all. When he found the Christians of Egypt still arguing about the Trinity, once again Athanasius got the blame. "That little nothing-man!" roared the Emperor. "That sly rascal! That born meddler! That odious puppet! Arrest him!"

But Athanasius was already on board a Nile boat, heading back to the desert. On the way, a police boat overtook him.

"Have you seen Athanasius?" yelled the police captain.

"Yes, he's just gone past," Athanasius called back. "You'll catch him if you hurry!"

An impatient shout had the oarsmen doubling their stroke, and the pursuers shot ahead, leaving Athanasius in their wake.

Hardly had he settled in his new exile, when two smiling monks brought him the news that Julian had been killed fighting in Persia. An army officer named Flavian was the new Emperor, and Flavian was a Catholic.

Unhappily, he died after only a few months, but the rest of his own life Athanasius lived out in comparative quiet. He was subjected to one more brief exile, when the pro-Arian policies of Valens, Flavian's successor, drove the Alexandrians to riot, but Valens soon called him back and he never had to leave Alexandria again.

Although he defended the truth so bravely, Athanasius was never arrogant; indeed, he was deeply conscious of his own limitations as a theologian. "The more I tried to make myself understand Christ's divine nature," he wrote, "the further away I seemed to be from the knowledge of it. And what little I did understand, I could not put down adequately in writing."

Many of those who veered towards Arianism did so, not out of disrespect for Our Lord, but because they did not want to diminish the honor due to God the Father. Athanasius was sympathetic to their difficulties, which often did boil down simply to questions of language.

Though he never became a monk, many of his friends thought that he was always one at heart, and few men did more, in those first days, to spread the monastic ideal. During his exile in Rome, he fired many people with enthusiasm for Antony's life-work, and after the desert saint died Athanasius wrote a biography—an early best-seller which is still our main source of information about him. It was to Athanasius, incidentally, that Antony left one of his two sheepskins.

Athanasius himself died peacefully on May 2, 373. Eight years later, at the second Council of Constantinople, Arianism was formally proscribed and all Arian office-holders removed.

Sinner, Heretic and Doctor of the Church

"Write whatever you know about the life and work of St. Augustine." If suddenly faced with so startling a demand, most of us, once we had recovered from our surprise, would be able to produce a few basic facts:

> Augustine, born in North Africa, lived an immoral life until, thanks to the prayers of his mother, St. Monica, he became a good Catholic. Later he was ordained priest, then bishop. He wrote a number of books including the Confessions, the story of his conversion.

No examiner could fault this, save on grounds of brevity. As far as it goes, it is perfectly correct. Yet, like most thumbnail sketches, it conceals the real man almost as effectively as total ignorance. In this case, it conceals the real woman also.

Augustine was born, on November 13th, 354, at Tagaste, which today is the Algerian town of Souk Ahras. Tagaste, one of Rome's tinier outposts, was 2,000 feet above sea-level and 200 miles inland. Until he was a college student Augustine never saw the sea. As a child he used to gaze into a glass of water, trying to imagine what it could be like.

His father, Patricius, was a pagan: a cheerful, generous man with a quick temper. Monica, his Christian wife, knew how to handle him, though; she would let him blow off steam and then, when he had quieted down, gently express her own point of view. More often than not he would admit that she was right. In a world where even middle-class husbands knocked their wives about as a matter of course, Monica was never seen with a bruise—a thing so remarkable that her friends, nursing their own battered faces, asked her how she managed it.

"Face the fact that as a wife, you have no more rights than a slave-girl," she told them drily. "When he's angry, never answer back." Some ladies, Augustine remembered, took the advice. Those who did not collected more bruises.

At school, Augustine himself collected plenty; the floggings that he got there left him with a lifelong distaste for corporal punishment and for violence of every kind. He was clever, even brilliant—his teachers soon saw that. He loved Latin and won a prize for rhetoric; his dramatic orations could move an audience to tears and applause. But he preferred playing ball to learning Greek, so Greek was beaten into him.

"No one does well what he does against his will," wrote Augustine ruefully in later life, and modern educators have made this the corner-stone of their philosophy. In fact, his whole attitude to education was remarkably modern: he believed that the free play of natural curiosity was a far better teacher than discipline and drill. All the same, as he freely admitted, he was glad that he was made to learn; for his painfully acquired education was to help him in ways that he could not then have dreamed of.

School must have seemed all the worse because he had been spoiled at home; like most parents who have them-

selves been over-strictly brought up, Monica was inclined to indulge her children (exactly how many she
had we do not know for certain, but it was not a large
family).

With a pagan husband she must have had some problems in bringing the little ones up as Christians, but at
least Patricius was tolerant. So Augustine was enrolled
as a catechumen, though not baptized. Monica, like most
women, had received little education: her own piety was
simple, but she gave Augustine a reverence for the name
of Jesus which never left him.

Augustine's parents were not rich, but they were both
strong-willed and ambitious for their boy. In the civil
service, he could go a long way; he certainly had the
right talents. Maybe he would even end up a provincial
governor. So they made a decision: Augustine would go to
college in Carthage.

There was, however, a snag. Since his father lacked the
necessary funds, Augustine had to spend a year kicking
his heels at home while Patricius scraped the money
together. Not surprisingly, he got into mischief, hanging
around the town with other lads and enjoying his first
sexual adventures.

Later, these adolescent sins caused Augustine much
remorse. In his *Confessions*, written when he was 45, he
torments himself with the memory of them. In particular,
he laments that he did not heed his mother's warnings to
keep himself pure.

Yet at this time he was only fifteen years old, unbaptized
and therefore cut off from the other Sacraments. He had
been subjected to a year's enforced idleness—a cruel
burden to lay on any youngster. He was surrounded by
bad example; his own father was frequently unfaithful,
as Augustine must have known. So were many other
husbands; infidelity was the accepted thing. As for

Monica's influence, she was ill-equipped to deal with his adolescent problems, as Augustine himself comes close to admitting. So, without wishing to make light of sexual sin, we cannot escape the feeling that the middle-aged bishop is being a little hard on the teenager when he goes on at extreme length about the "rottenness" and the "monstrousness" of his youthful escapades.

The sin which caused him most remorse, however, had nothing to do with sex. This was the famous—or notorious—episode of the pears.

"There was a pear-tree near our vineyard," Augustine recalled with sorrow. "The fruit on it was plentiful, but not much good. Yet some of us young tearaways, after we had been hanging round the streets until late at night, as we usually did, went round there and shook a huge load of pears off the tree. Not because we wanted to eat them, oh no! We only took a few bites. The rest of the fruit we threw to the hogs."

Raiding an orchard is something many of us have done as youngsters without suffering excessive guilt-pangs in adult life. Yet once again Augustine reproaches himself for pages—simply because, he says, this sin was committed for the love of the sin itself, not for love of the pears or to gain any other apparent good. He sees it as something akin to the rebellion of Lucifer. Most of us will see only a stupid act of vandalism committed by a group of bored youths.

He continued his wild life during his student days in Carthage—at least, he thought that it was wild and it might seem so to us, but it was no better and no worse than the behavior of most of the young men around him.

Now two things happened which affected him deeply. His father Patricius died, having become a Christian not long before. And Augustine fell in love.

We know nothing about the girl; not even her name.

We do not know why he never married her, for they lived together for many years and she bore him a son. Perhaps she was married already; more probably she was a slave, or anyway someone too low in the social scale to be the wife of a rising young professional man.

Surely Monica, the devout Catholic, was shocked and disturbed by the relationship? Apparently not. Probably she considered a concubine the least of several possible evils. She knew that marriage, for the moment at least, was out of the question. She knew that her clever son was highly sexed and inclined to be irresponsible. Maybe a stable relationship—even an irregular one—would have a good effect, help to settle him down, prepare him for a proper Christian marriage in due course. We cannot say for sure that those were her views, but it seems likely.

What disturbed her very much more—in fact, it came as a major shock—was to find that Augustine had become a Manichaean heretic. How could it have happened? How could her beloved boy have arrived among this strange and sinister sect, whose organized secret cells were spreading like a cancer across the Empire?

When Augustine arrived in Carthage to begin his college studies, it was, as we know, with a definite object in view. He was going to qualify for a civil service post and so become one of the mandarin class which ran the Empire.

Then he read a book which made him think again about his whole future: Cicero's *Hortensius*, which exhorted thinking men to the study of philosophy. Here, Augustine realized, lay his true vocation. He would become not an administrator but an academic, a teacher. He would devote himself to the intellectual life.

At about this time, also, he read another book, one which impressed him far less: the Bible. Written in simple Greek, it struck him as naive and childish. Its message left him cold. In both style and content, it seemed much inferior to Cicero.

His main complaint was that it failed to solve the problem of evil, in particular as it applied to himself. If he, Augustine, wished to be good, why did he continue to commit sin? Why did God allow him to go on committing it? Was God Himself really good?

Yes indeed, said the Manichees, God was good; but He was not in full control. There was in the world a principle of evil, just as powerful as God; good and evil were mixed in the world and mixed in every human person, for all matter was evil and our bodies were matter. If a man sinned, therefore, it was not really he who sinned but the evil principle in him. Only by following a vigorous code of self-denial, including abstinence from meat and sexual intercourse, could a man hope to liberate the good in him from the evil.

A few privileged Manichees, known as the "elect", achieved this. The rest, known as "hearers", might aspire to it, but for the moment they need not follow the ascetic code and, of course, need not worry about their sins, for to do so was pointless.

Small wonder that Augustine found this doctrine attractive. With its fine philosophical ring, it flattered his intellectual vanity. At the same time, it excused his way of life.

When Augustine arrived home in Tagaste and told his mother that he was now a "hearer", she forbade him to enter her house.

For the next nine years, while Augustine taught school, Monica wore him and everyone else out with her prayers, her pleading and her weeping. Again and again she visited the local bishop for solace until, in a fit of holy exasperation, he assured her, in a phrase that became famous, that "the son of so many tears could not perish."

You will by now have gathered that the popular picture of Monica as a naturally serene and gentle lady, patiently waiting on God's mercy, is not accurate. She was tough, determined, and more than a shade hysterical. For Monica, as for Augustine, the road to sainthood was not easy.

In 383, Augustine left for Rome. He had established his reputation as a philosophy professor, first in Tagaste, then in Carthage. Now it was time to move to the big city. He sailed secretly after tricking his mother into believing that he would stay in Carthage. When, in the morning, she found that he was gone, her cries on the quayside were terrible.

She followed him, as he must have known she would. By now he had grown disillusioned with Manichaeism; he had found it shallow and no answer to his problems. While her son was in an intellectual vacuum. Monica was confident that he would return to Catholicism. A dream had revealed it to her, and she set great store by her dreams.

They did not stay in Rome, for in Rome, he discovered, students were quick to learn but slow to pay. Offered a chance to teach in Milan, he took it with both hands, for Milan was now a most important place where the Western Emperor had his residence. At this time, though he did not yet know it, he had reached the turning-point in his life. For in Milan, at last, he was baptized.

Two great influences helped to bring him back to his mother's religion. First, he read the books of the neoplatonist philosophers—men who argued, with great skill and sophistication, the supremacy of God and the primacy of the supernatural over the material. Here he found the intellectual conviction which the Manichees had failed to provide. There was, his new teachers assured him, no evil principle fighting God on equal terms.

Evil was simply the absence of good—the good to which all men might come if they would look honestly into their own souls.

Looking, of course, was simply the first step; Augustine realized it only too well. As a youngster he had prayed: "Lord, make me pure, but not yet," and this was still the problem. He knew what to do, but he lacked the willpower to do it.

The second great influence on him was not a book, or a philosophical system, but a person. Ambrose, the Bishop of Milan, was a saint. Some saints are warm and approachable, others are awe-inspiring. Ambrose was the second kind.

He had been a Roman governor; the people had elected him bishop by popular acclaim. Within eight days, the unbaptized layman was celebrating his first Pontifical Mass. He negotiated with Emperors, he composed Latin hymns which are sung to this day; by his ministry among the governing class, he secured the Western Empire for the Church.

Yet his door was always open; not even the poorest ever had to make an appointment to see him. Augustine, when he called, would sometimes find the great man reading. Then he would stand in a corner of the room, just watching, unwilling to disturb his studies.

The books Ambrose read were those which Augustine himself devoured; for Ambrose also was an ardent neo-platonist and he constantly wove the thought of Plotinus and the other philosophers into his preaching. Again and again in his sermons, Ambrose would urge the value of self-denial, the discipline of the soul. So highly did he praise virginity that some families, anxious to promote a good marriage, would not permit their daughters to listen to him.

At first, Augustine had gone to hear Ambrose partly out

of professional interest, to study his technique. Soon he
was captivated, and at the same time, disturbed. For the
bishop's constant emphasis on self-denial only shar-
pened his own inner tensions.

During these long years of searching, his mistress and
their son had been with him constantly. Now, with brutal
suddenness, she was torn from his side. It was, I need
hardly say, Monica's doing. Augustine, she pointed out,
could scarcely hope for baptism, let alone marriage,
while he was living in sin. Monica had a fiancée lined
up: unfortunately she was rather young at present, so
Augustine would have to wait for two years. Meanwhile,
the concubine must go. Augustine acquiesced. He had
always known that their relationship could not go on for
ever. And yet . . .

"My heart clung to her," wrote the bishop, years later.
"She left it torn and wounded and bleeding. She went
back to Africa promising never to take any other man,
either as husband or lover. Our son she left with me."

The amputation was necessary; we can only wish that
it had been performed more humanely. Did she have to
go back to Africa, this faithful young woman? Their son,
her son, was only 15— just the age Augustine had been
during that terrible year of idleness in Tagaste. Did anyone think of him? With little surprise we learn that Augustine swiftly found solace in the arms of another
woman.

His conflict, however, was drawing towards its crisis.
A friend told him the story of two men who had been
converted to God's service by reading Athanasius's biography of Antony. Augustine was deeply troubled—
partly, he realized to his astonishment, by professional
pride.

"What are we doing," he asked his bosom friend,
Alypius, "to let men without any education conquer

Heaven by force, while we, with all our learning, hang around like this?

With surprise Alypius realized that Augustine was close to tears. At that moment they were sitting together in a small garden; Augustine, too overcome to continue the conversation, got up and walked away while Alypius looked after him.

There was a fig-tree nearby; Augustine flung himself down beneath it and prayed, almost frantically: "How long, Lord, do I have to wait? How long are you going to leave me in my sins?"

Suddenly he heard a voice: not Alypius calling him, but a child's voice, coming from a house nearby. *"Tolle lege,"* it chanted, over and over. *"Tolle lege."* Take up and read.

Augustine, lifted his head, puzzled. He knew no children's game that contained those words. Momentarily, the thought of Antony flashed across his mind. Antony had been converted by a single verse of scripture! Suppose . . . suppose he were to obey that childish suggestion—or was it an order?

He ran back to Alypius, who by now was even more surprised, and snatched up a copy of St. Paul's letters from the spot where he had laid it down. Once, he had despised the Scriptures. How different it all was now! Opening the book with trembling fingers, he found himself looking at the 13th chapter of the Letter to the Romans.

"Have nothing more to do with drunkenness, fights, illicit love affairs, quarrels or envious thoughts; make the Lord Jesus Christ your armor and do not indulge your passions any more."

Augustine read no further—there was no need. Alypius, too, had been trembling on the brink of Baptism: at the Easter Vigil Mass on April 24th, 387, they were both baptized by Bishop Ambrose, along with young Adeodatus, Augustine's son. Who the little singer had been, Augustine never discovered.

"Too late have I loved thee, O beauty so ancient and so new, too late have I loved thee!" We have all read Augustine's famous lament for the wasted years of his youth. Now he was to make up for them.

With Alypius and a group of friends, he resolved to return to Africa and found a religious Community. During the days spent waiting for a ship at the seaport of Ostia, Augustine and Monica stood one evening at a window looking into an enclosed garden—and there, briefly, they glimpsed together the happiness of Heaven. That Monica should have been allowed to share this mystical experience with her son was surely a reward for all her prayers and her weeping. Nine days later she died, serene and happy, quite untroubled that her bones were to lie far from her beloved Africa.

Augustine returned to his home town and set up his community. There, two years later, Adeodatus died. Augustine had loved the boy dearly, as he had loved the faithful woman who bore him. Now God had taken him—and with him Augustine's last family tie.

It had never been his intention to enter the priesthood, but in those days—as we saw in the case of Ambrose—a vocation was not always an inner calling. If the Christian community chose a man to be priest or bishop, then priest or bishop he became. The voice of the people was the voice of God.

In Hippo, Africa's second largest port, Bishop Valerius needed an assistant. His people chose Augustine. Five years later, in 396, Augustine succeeded him.

As a bishop, he took great care of the poor; he fed them and handed out clothes once a year, sometimes going into debt to provide relief. To raise the ransom-money for captives he would, if necessary, melt down sacred vessels.

Life in Augustine's palace was no miserable affair; the repentant sinner still knew how to enjoy himself. Always fond of company, he sometimes caused a mild flutter by asking pagans to dinner. No such invitation went to Catholics whose lives were scandalous. There was always wine, but nobody was allowed more than his fair share. Anyone who swore was "fined" one cup!

Backbiting was never tolerated. In the dining-room Augustine had hung a sign which said:"If anyone wants to speak ill of his neighbour, this table is not the place for him." Once, when an offender refused to desist, Augustine jumped up. "Either that sign goes or I do!" he said.

He lived in Community with his clergy and he also founded a convent of nuns. A letter which he wrote to them, together with two sermons on the subject, form the "Rule" on which several of the great religious Orders later based their lives.

His sermons, of which about 500 survive, were often received with an exuberance which would startle a modern bishop. "I am glad that you shouted," he said one day. "It shows that you know the Scriptures." On another occasion, noticing that some of the congregation looked jaded, he called a break for refreshments.

Augustine complained sadly that pastoral cares left him so little time for thought and writing; yet today, more than 15 centuries after his death, he is still a major force in Christian thought. Like Paul, he did most of his work in response to the needs of the moment and often as a reply to heretics: not only his old Manichaean colleagues, but also the Donatists and the Pelagians, both of them powerful in his day.

Donatists, who gained much ground in Africa, held

that the Church, by departing from its traditions, had forfeited its divine mission. Only they themselves had remained true and were, therefore, the authentic remnant of the Church which Christ founded.

The Pelagians, led by a British monk, said in effect that we can get to Heaven by our own efforts; we have only to make the right moral decisions—grace is not necessary. (This heresy is, of course, also very modern in tone).

In response to both these very different heresies, Augustine produced what he considered his most important work: *The City of God.* The book drew a picture of two invisible societies, the elect and the damned. Nobody knows who belongs to which save God, who knows from all eternity who will receive the necessary grace.

In fact Augustine appears to say, here and elsewhere, that we are saved or damned before we are born and that we can do nothing to alter our destiny. His doctrine of predestination has never been accepted by the Church, which has always insisted on the role of free-will.

Less controversial, yet no less profound, are his writings on Scripture and also his work on the Trinity, which owes so much to his beloved neoplatonists. By his use of Greek thought, he paved the way for the Christian thinkers of the Middle Ages. Yet the *Confessions*, his most popular work, he wrote for the simplest of reasons: to stop men from over-praising him and to encourage others to amend their lives.

Augustine died on August 28, 430. The Roman Empire was in its last agony. Already the Vandal invaders were pouring across North Africa; the great Christian Church which had flourished there was swiftly destroyed. A year after Augustine's death Hippo was evacuated; soon afterwards the Vandals entered and burned it to the ground.

Ireland's Fiery Arrow

The Catholic Church, we are often told, treats women as second-class citizens. Since she is, undeniably, ruled by men, the charge—whether true or not—is inevitable.

Perhaps that is why God sends, from time to time, women saints whose impact on the Church can only be called dynamic, who dazzlingly outshine their male contemporaries. Saints like Brigid, who is, after Patrick himself, the most important figure in all the long history of Irish Christianity.

Like all the earlier saints, she was canonized long ago by popular acclaim—which is just as well, for she would fare badly in a modern canonization process. Nobody doubts for a moment that she was indeed a very great saint. The trouble is, there is so little hard evidence to prove it. There are folk tales aplenty. There are several ancient biographies, long on piety but short on facts, and sometimes contradicting one another—hardly the sort of "evidence" to satisfy canon lawyers who have to protect the Communion of Saints from gatecrashers.

Nevertheless, from these uncertain sources, a remarkably vivid picture emerges. More importantly, not only is it vivid, it is also consistent. "Yes," we think, again and again. "I can just see her. I know exactly what she must have been like."

Reading the old stories, the old biographies, is rather like looking at a picture by one of the great Impressionist painters—Monet, say, or Cezanne. From those deliberately-blurred outlines, those cunningly-placed blocks of color, there emerges a reality which is more true than any photograph could hope to be.

So, while most Celtic saints are lost in the mists of time, Brigid lives. All over Europe, all over the U.S., churches bear her name. Every year tiny Brigids, Bridgets, Brigittes and Brigits are baptized by the hundred. When Eire's television network, Telefis Eireann, wanted a station symbol, it chose the rush cross which Brigid once wove at a sick man's bedside.

What was she really like, then, this 5th-Century Irishwoman who is still so richly remembered? Well, we do have a few solid facts. Brigid began life as an illegitimate slave-girl. She was born, around the year 453, at Faughart, near Dundalk, in County Louth. Her father, Dubthach, was a pagan chieftain; her mother, Brocessa, one of his Christian slaves.

Possibly Dubthach's wife was upset by the pregnancy. At any rate, she took a dislike to Brocessa and insisted that her husband sell her. Brocessa's new owner was a druid who lived many miles away, in the west.

She took the baby with her, but as soon as Brigid was old enough her father, the chieftain Dubthach, claimed her back; under the law he had that right. So Brigid found herself working for him: tending his sheep and pigs, grinding his corn, cooking and waiting at table.

She was a slave, as her mother had been before her, but she had the instincts of a queen. No leper or beggar, coming to the door, left without a hand-out; even stray dogs were fed—if necessary with food from the chieftain's table.

Maybe we should spare a thought for Dubthach and,

more especially, for his wife. Having Brigid around the place must have been a strain—a constant reminder of her husband's infidelity. The girl's compulsive generosity would surely have aggravated her past all bearing.

When Brigid was told, one morning, to prepare for a journey in the chieftain's chariot, apparently she thought that it was some kind of treat. "It is not to honor you that I am taking you," her father scowled. "You are being sold to the King of Leinster." Once again, Mrs. Dubthach had spoken.

Outside the wattle-and-daub palace, Brigid was told to wait while her father went in to announce their arrival. Whatever thoughts were going through Brigid's head at that moment, they were swiftly interrupted. A face was peering at her over the chariot-rim: a hideous face, rotting and twisted. A leper's face.

"Alms, lady," the leper whined piteously.

Brigid looked around. No money or food here, yet to turn the man away would be unthinkable. Suddenly, a gleam of metal caught her eye. Her father's sword! Ornate, highly-polished, razor-sharp—if the poor fellow sold that he would get enough money to keep him going for weeks. Without a moment's hesitation, she gave it to him.

What a moral theologian would make of her action, I cannot say. On the face of it, the sword was not hers to give. Yet her father could soon get another; he was, after all, a chieftain. The leper, on the other hand, depended on charity for his very existence. If people were not generous to him, he starved.

Brigid, in any case, did not stop to weigh the moral pros and cons. Neither did the leper. Seizing the sword, he hobbled off as rapidly as his poor crippled legs could carry him.

Dubthach came out, discovered what had happened,

and howled with rage. Did she not realize that the sword
was valuable—that it had cost many gold pieces? Yes, of
course, replied Brigid. That was why she had given it to
Jesus. Dubthach gave up. Quite plainly the girl was
mad. He thanked his own gods that he was getting rid of
her.

Now the king was, as it happened, a Christian—one of
St. Patrick's own converts. He understood Brigid's thinking, even if her pagan father did not.

"Leave her alone," he said. "God is more pleased with
her than he is with you or me."

Dubthach swallowed hard. The king was his over-
lord—better not argue. The upshot of the episode was
that, instead of becoming the king's slave, Brigid got her
freedom.

Since his daughter was now, so to speak, one of the
family, the harassed chieftain dutifully set about trying
to arrange a good marriage for her. Brigid, with the utmost kindness, turned the young man down. Nothing
personal, she assured him. He was a fine young fellow
and he would soon get an attractive wife; to assist him in
his search, she promised him her prayers and gave him
some sound advice about his courting technique! As for
herself, she was already promised. She was going to become a bride of Christ.

This did not mean going into a convent, for in Ireland
no convents existed. In those far-off days, a woman who
wanted to live as a consecrated virgin remained in her
own home, her vows a matter solely between herself and
God. If it was a pagan home, as it was in Brigid's case,
then she might well have a hard time, enduring the jeers
and the hostility of her family. Patrick, in his travels,
often marvelled at the courage of such women.

In the Egyptian desert, Pachomius had quickly seen

the need for community life. Pachomius was a military man; his mind ran naturally along those lines.

Brigid had no such background: yet instinctively she saw that this was what the women religious of Ireland needed. At Fertullagh in Westmeath, she and seven friends took their vows formally before Bishop Mel of Offaly. From then on they lived together—and the first Irish convent had been formed.

Exactly where these first Sisters lived has never been established precisely; anyway, the point is of small interest because Brigid spent the rest of her life traveling the length and breadth of Ireland setting up new foundations. By the time she died, no fewer than 13,000 nuns were living in established communities there.

For most of her life, her headquarters were at Kildare (*Cill-dara*, the Cell of the Oak), where the King of Leinster gave her land. From the first small dwelling under the oaktree there grew, like an oak from an acorn, an abbey so large that in the end it became a small township.

Not only was there a covent for women; soon Brigid found herself establishing a monastery for men who wanted to live a religious life on the same pattern as her nuns. They had their own superior, but he answered to Brigid, who remained in overall control.

It became clear that a bishop was needed to confirm, ordain and preach. Close to the abbey lived Conlaeth, a hermit of great holiness. Brigid asked him to become their bishop. Even had he wished to refuse, he must have realised that it would be useless. Once Brigid had made her mind up, that was it! So Conlaeth moved to the abbey, to look after its members and the lay people who lived around it.

That a bishop should be chosen by a mother superior and that he should function under her jurisdiction may come as a surprise, especially to those who accuse the Church of male chauvinism, but so it was at Kildare.

Prayer was, of course, the basic reason for the abbey's existence, but both monks and nuns were totally self-supporting and spent many hours a day both in the care of the poor and in the work with which they supported themselves.

Chalices, crucifixes, bells and illustrated books poured from Kildare to all parts of Ireland. The monastery was, in fact, the country's first industrial complex.

Over this great institution, when she was not on her travels, Brigid ruled with kindness, wisdom and great good humor. She was never too grand to take a turn with the milking, the corn-grinding, the butter-churning and the many other tasks of house and farm; and it is a reasonable guess that her mind must often have gone back, while she was about her tasks, to the days when she was a slave-girl.

She had long ago managed to secure her mother's freedom; indeed, that had been her first concern, once she herself was free. The story goes that Brocessa's druid master and his wife both became Christians after Brigid miraculously replaced butter which she had taken from the druidical dairy and given to the poor!

This uncaring generosity remained one of her basic character-traits; to the end of her days she went on giving regardless of anything but the needs of the poor. It is said that Conlaeth, returning from a visit to Rome, brought back a set of rich vestments which he loved to wear. When he went to the sacristy one day, however, the vestments had disappeared. Brigid had given them away to raise funds for the beggars who regularly beseiged the abbey gates. Poor Conlaeth! It was useless to complain. He just had to grit his teeth.

Her generosity is commemorated to this day in some of

Ireland's country districts, where people still put out bread and porridge for the saint on "St. Brigid's Night" (her feast is February 1st).

But the most popular Brigid custom is, of course, the rush cross so familiar to Ireland's television viewers. The story goes that Brigid was asked to visit a pagan chieftain who was seriously ill and whom some of his friends hoped to convert to Christianity. When she arrived at the house, however, the patient was so delirious that there was no possibility of giving him any sort of instruction. Brigid, sitting down by the bed, began to talk to him gently; as she talked, she absent-mindedly picked up some rushes from the floor and began to weave them into a cross by fastening the ends together. The sick man, lucid for a moment, asked her what she was doing. Brigid explained the meaning of the cross, and the chieftain, now calm, questioned her so eagerly that he soon knew enough to want Baptism.

There is every reason to believe the story true. The strength of the custom is a powerful argument, and it seems entirely plausible that Brigid's serene presence would have a calming, therapeutic effect on the patient.

At least one of the many miracle stories also has a distinct ring of truth, simply because it shows Brigid acting so very much in character. Lepers were especially dear to her, and she was often credited with curing them. Once, two came together to seek her help, and she told them to wash each other in turn.

The first man rinsed down his friend, who was promptly made whole. But the friend did not return the service; though he himself had only just been healed, he shrunk from touching someone who still had the dread disease. Instead of berating the man for his stupid ingratitude, Brigid calmly washed the other leper herself, and he too was cured.

Some of her reputed miracles are distinctly humorous; for example, the fate she is said to have visited on two robbers who stole cattle from the abbey fields at night. They got them as far as a river which had to be forded—and there the animals dug their heels in and refused to cross. No amount of whacking or yelling made any difference, so at daybreak the men decided to try to pull them to the other side with ropes.

They stripped, tied their clothes to the animals' horns, and pulled hard. At first it looked as though they would succeed but in midstream, the cattle broke away and galloped back towards the abbey. The local peasants, just getting up, rubbed their eyes at the sight of the cattle, clothes flapping from their horns, galloping across the fields with two naked robbers in desperate pursuit.

Only once in her life does Brigid ever appear to have been angry, and then it was with two of her own nuns. During one of her many visitations, she and her two companions arrived during Lent at a convent where they were, as always, joyfully received.

Soon they were conducted into the convent refectory and there, awaiting them, was a meal of bread and bacon. Now this came as a surprise, for as a general rule, Celtic convents abstained from all forms of meat during Lent. Nevertheless, Brigid sat down and began to eat with obvious enjoyment.

It did not take her long to realize that her companions were prissily and pointedly *not* enjoying their meal; they were leaving their bacon untouched. Brigid promptly rose and bundled the pair of them out of the room, leaving them to meditate on the overriding importance of courtesy and charity.

Ascetic though she was, Brigid loved life and its gifts. She had Francis of Assisi's devotion to animals, and it was said that they came to her unbidden as they came to him. (The patron of all dairy-maids, she is often pictured along with a cow.)

Once, says legend, she used her animal magic to save from execution a poor man who had inadvertently killed a Chieftain's pet fox. Calling a wild fox from the woods, she taught it an extensive repertoire of tricks and presented it to the chieftain, who promptly relented.

She was a woman of immensely varied talents. If she was not the only saint who brewed beer, she is certainly the only one credited with a devotional poem on the subject:

> I should like a great lake of ale
> For the King of the Kings.
> I should like the family of heaven
> To be drinking it through time eternal . . .
>
> I should like cheerfulness
> To be in their drinking;
> I should like Jesus,
> Too, to be there among them.
>
> I should like the three
> Marys of illustrious renown;
> I should like the people
> Of heaven there from all parts . . .

The beer which Brigid brewed was, I hasten to say, not the kind that one would imbibe in a present-day bar. The beer which remained a staple drink throughout the Middle Ages was scarcely fermented and its alcoholic content was extremely low. No one can prove with certainty that she wrote the poem. I, for one, hope she did, though. It perfectly illustrates her spirit: her love of God, her warmth towards others, her never-failing hospitality.

Brigid died in 525 and was buried, with Conlaeth, in

front of the high altar at the great church in Kildare. In later centuries, the shrine was much desecrated, first by Norse invaders and later by Ireland's Protestant rulers. During the 16th Century her remains were secretly removed to save them from a worse fate, and nobody knows for certain where they lie today. Her head, however, found its way, via Austria, to Lisbon—an unlikely resting-place for a saint who never once left Ireland.

Nevertheless, once she was dead her cult spread through Europe like wildfire. At one time, it was said, every major cathedral there had a shrine to Brigid or commemorated her in some way.

The fervor of the Irish themselves has at times been startling. In the Middle Ages, they did not hesitate to compare her to Our Lady— as in this beautiful passage from the *Book of Lismore*:

> For everything that Brigid would ask of the Lord was granted her at once. For this was her desire: to satisfy the poor, to expel every hardship, to spare every miserable man . . .

> She was abstemious, she was innocent, she was prayerful, she was patient. She was glad in God's commandments; she was firm, she was humble, she was forgiving, she was loving; she was a consecrated casket for keeping Christ's body and His blood: she was a temple of God. Her heart and mind were a throne of rest for the Holy Spirit. She was simple to God; she was compassionate to the wretched; she was splended in miracles and marvels.

> Wherefore her name among created things is dove among birds, vine among trees, sun among stars . . .

It is she that helps everyone in difficulty or danger; it is she who abates pestilences; it is she who quells the anger and storm of the sea. She is the prophetess of Christ; she is the Queen of the South: she is the Mary of the Gael.

Extravagant? Possibly. Brigid would certainly have thought so. "Can that really be me they are talking about?" We hear her ask, in amused disbelief. Yet she would, surely, clap her hands with delight to see her rush cross on the television screen, and the food so lovingly left out on her feast.

Today Brigid is one of Ireland's patron saints, the only one actually born in the country. Yet she belongs to us all, even those with no drop of Irish blood.

Her name means "fiery arrow", and that is what she was—an arrow shot on that day at Fertullagh when she and her companions took their vows. The fire which they started burns on today in every land Irish nuns work for the Church.

The Man Who
Changed Europe

Shortly before the year 500, a young man from the Italian countryside arrived in Rome to attend college. With him came his childhood nurse.

We can easily imagine what kind of reception would await an able-bodied freshman arriving at an American college with a nurse in tow, but in 6th-Century Rome such an arrangement raised fewer eyebrows.

The young law student, whose name was Benedict, did not like the Eternal City which, indeed, was in a sorry state.

The last of the Caesars had gone. The Western Empire was ruled from Ravenna by the Ostrogoth invader Theodoric. Disorder and immorality were rife; at that very moment there was an undignified squabble over the Throne of Peter which Theodoric eventually had to settle. Benedict, who felt called to the monastic life, looked forward increasingly to the day when he could leave college and serve God in solitude.

In fact, he never did complete his college studies. Finding Rome unbearable, he moved with his nurse to Affile, 35 miles away in the mountains, where he lived for a time with a group of ascetics. His final departure to the wilderness was precipitated by, of all unlikely things, a broken colander.

The old nurse, wanting to prepare a tasty dish for her charge, had borrowed the colander from a neighbour. During her cooking, it slipped from her hands on to the floor and broke in two.

Moved by her floods of tears, Benedict did what he could to console her, then knelt down and prayed. Miraculously, the colander was made whole again. Though Benedict urged her to silence, the old woman could not contain her excitement. *"Un santo!"* she cried, again and again, running through the streets bearing the colander aloft. "A saint!"

Benedict, unable to bear the adulation which followed, left Rome hurriedly with the nurse in hot pursuit.

That, anyway, is the story which Pope Gregory the Great was told when, 50 years after Benedict's death, he set to work on a short biography. (Strange how often one saint writes another's life!) And there must have been some foundation for it because, Gregory assures us, a colander was venerated for many years in Affile's Church of St. Peter.

Benedict's stay with the ascetics—a loosely-organized community, probably of both sexes—did not last long.

Five miles from Affile lay a rocky gorge with the River Anio running through it. In this wild place, called Subiaco, many solitaries had already found a home, for the steep rock-faces were riddled with caves. Here Benedict apprenticed himself to a holy man named Romanus. His need, he explained, was for maximum solitude; Romanus found him a vacant cave under an overhanging rock, so difficult of access that bread was lowered to him on a rope. He clothed Benedict in the regulation sheepskin, and the young man, now an accredited hermit, clambered down the rock-face and took up residence.

For a time he was left undisturbed; his only contact was Romanus, his spiritual director, who also brought his food. Then, just as Antony had done before him, he began to have visitors.

The first came as a pleasant surprise. A kindly priest, sitting down to dinner on Easter Sunday, suddenly thought of the lonely hermit marooned in his raven's nest of a cell. Gathering up the food from the table, he packed it into a bag and was soon scrambling down the incredibly steep path leading to Benedict's eyrie.

"Don't you know what day it is?" he asked the surprised Benedict. "Even you can't fast today!"

The two men dined together, and when it was time for the priest to go, each felt that it was the best Easter he had ever had.

Soon afterwards a group of shepherds scrambled down to get the holy man's blessing. At first, catching sight of his sheepskin among the bushes, they had imagined him to be some strange animal! Benedict felt he could not let them go without a few words of spiritual advice. Then other devout people began to come. Some made it down to the cave; others contented themselves with shouting from above. They brought food and got guidance and prayers in return.

Benedict was fast learning the lesson that Antony learned in the desert. Become holy on your own, and the world will beat a path to your door.

He learned, too, that the cave in the rocks is no hiding-place from difficulty or temptation. The memory of a girl he had known began to fill his imagination and, no matter how hard he prayed, kept on coming back. He began to doubt himself. Perhaps he was not, after all, suited to this solitary life. Perhaps he ought to forget his search for God and return to the world.

Realizing what was happening to him, he decided on drastic action. Outside the cave, on a ledge in the rock face, was a thick clump of briars. Throwing off his sheepskin, Benedict rolled himself in it.

His reputation grew steadily, not only among layfolk but among his fellow-hermits. A few miles away, at a spot called Vicovaro, lived a group of men, half-hermits and half-monks, who lived together in separate huts and yet met regularly for prayer and for spiritual direction from an abbot whom they had elected from their number. One day the abbot died. Who, they asked themselves, could take his place? It did not take them long to come up with an answer.

When the deputation came scrambling down the cliff-face Benedict was taken aback. When he had come out to Subiaco, it was certainly not with the intention of becoming anyone's leader, and in any case, he did not feel in tune with their life-style. Surely they ought to look elsewhere. It was useless; the men of Vicovaro had an answer for every argument. Here they were, sheep needing a shepherd. And no one was better qualified than Benedict.

In the end, reluctantly, he gave way and moved down to the flat land where Vicovaro stood. Sizing up his new charges, he soon realized that they needed some drastic changes in their way of life. Self-will, eccentricity, unhealthy introspection . . . the diseases of solitude were plainly present, and the only answer was a more disciplined and tightly-knit Community. So he reduced the number of penitential practices, and the amount of time given to them, and introduced a set order of the day.

There was nothing revolutionary about this. Even in Italy, there were established, before Benedict's time, monasteries where men lived a full Community life. Nevertheless, the hermits of Vicovaro reacted violently. Who did this fellow Benedict think he was, imposing rules and time-tables on them? They were hermits, not monks!

Resentment grew. If Benedict noticed it, he ignored it. Finally, the rebels' anger reached flashpoint and the fateful words were spoken. Benedict must be removed.

But the hermits, having no constitution, had no means of deposing an unpopular abbot. So, having begged him to lead them, they decided to kill him

A cup of wine was, as usual, brought to Benedict at the evening meal. But this time it was poisoned. As he raised his hand to bless it, the cup shattered and the poison spilled on the ground. Benedict looked his would-be murderers in the eye.

"I came here reluctantly," he said. "At your insistence. Now I will stay with you no longer. Find yourselves an abbot after your own hearts." And with that he turned his back upon them.

The most difficult part of the story, for many of us, is not the miracle but the poison attempt. Would men who had chosen a God-centered life actually try to kill an unpopular superior?

Two things need to be remembered. First, these were rough and violent days, when sudden death was taken much more for granted than it is today. Secondly, the monks of Vicovaro had fasted long and driven themselves hard, without adequate direction. Quite probably, some of them had become unbalanced. Crazy with pride, they imagined that in killing Benedict they were doing God's work.

The whole horrible experience might have been expected to turn Benedict away from Community-style monasticism. Instead, it was the prelude to his life work.

Before long, he had established a whole chain of monasteries at Subiaco: small Communities, usually of ten men, with the tenth, the *decanus*, acting as superior.

In setting up small monasteries, Benedict was following a tradition already established. But those at Subiaco were not independent; Benedict remained in overall charge, each *decanus* reporting to him.

The new Community flourished mightily. Young men flocked there, eager to offer their lives to God. The layfolk came from miles around to attend Mass at Subiaco and to seek the monks' counsel.

This lay enthusiasm led to fresh trouble—and to an unexpected move. In those days the parish clergy were not as carefully chosen or as carefully trained as they are today. The priest in whose parish Subiaco was located seems to have been a psychopath.

Finding his own church deserted, he went mad with jealousy and mounted a diabolical campaign against the monks. To distract them from their prayers, he sent a troupe of local girls to dance erotically outside their cells; and when that had no effect he made an attempt on Benedict's life. Once again, poisoning was the means chosen. The priest sent Benedict a gift of poisoned bread, but instinctively Benedict knew that something was wrong and did not eat it.

Though he had escaped once again, he realized that something must be done to heal the situation. The monks must have peace at all costs, or how could they carry on their work of prayer? Since the hostility was mainly directed against himself, Benedict decided to leave and found a new monastery elsewhere. Placing Subiaco in charge of his trusted assistant, Maurus, he set out with a group of young monks for Monte Cassino, a mountain roughly halfway between Rome and Naples.

Why he chose Monte Cassino we do not know. Perhaps

the local bishop, or some other influential admirer, invited him. Whatever the reason, the choice proved a historic one. For there on the hilltop the monks built themselves a house on the site of a pagan temple; and there the monks of St. Benedict have lived ever since.

Not continuously, for Benedict prophesied that his monastery would be destroyed three times, and his prophecy has been fulfilled. In 589, barely 40 years after his death, the Lombards attacked it. Almost 400 years later, it was the turn of the Saracens. Finally, on February 15, 1944, the monastery again suffered destruction during bitter fighting between Allied and German troops. Yet each time, a new and greater abbey has risen from the ashes of the old, and Monte Cassino remains the mother-house of Western monasticism.

In a tower which has miraculously survived each destruction, Benedict spent the rest of his life in comparative peace, despite the civil turmoil which continued to tear Italy apart. Though he taught his monks not to become involved in worldly affairs, Benedict also taught—and practised—the utmost compassion to those who were suffering, and the poor always knew that they would find a welcome at Monte Cassino. In time of famine, the monks would themselves go without bread in order to feed their neighbours.

Once a young cleric named Agapitus came to the monastery to beg a little oil for his soup. He was starving; the soup was little more than water.

The monks themselves had only a tiny spot of oil left in the bottom of a jar, but Benedict ordered the cellarer to give it to Agapitus. The cellarer, deciding that Benedict had gone mad, sent word that they had no oil to give.

A little later, Benedict inquired whether his order had been carried out. The cellarer flushed with embarrassment. He knew that Benedict would see through any lie.

"Father, I could not!" he blurted. "If I had given the oil away, there would have been no dinner for the monks."

Benedict was rarely angry, but when he was, his anger was terrible.

"Bring me the oil-jar," he thundered.

Cowed, the trembling Brother brought it. As the Brothers watched in disbelief, their abbot flung the earthenware jar out of the window. Bumping and banging down the hillside, hitting rock after rock—surely it must shatter, and the last of the oil spill on to the parched earth!

But no—though their eyes could scarcely credit it, the jar remained intact.

"Now," said Benedict calmly. "Take the jar to Agapitus."

This time the cellarer did as he was told. Benedict, meanwhile, told the rest of the monks to follow him down to the cellar. There, before an empty oil-jar, he knelt down and led them in prayer.

If any of them wondered what was happening, they knew better than to ask. In any case, they had not long to wait, for before their eyes the jar slowly filled up with oil—enough to last for many days.

On another occasion, two Brothers who had been sent on a journey were invited by a friend of the monks to stay and have a meal with her. It was against the monastery rule to dine out, but the monks succumbed. On their return, Benedict immediately told them with whom they had dined and how many cups of wine they had enjoyed. He did not impose a penance. The shock, he felt, was sufficient.

Again, when another friend of the monastery sent two flasks of wine as a present for the founder, the servant

entrusted with them decided to keep one for himself. He
hid it in bushes beside the path to the monastery, intending to enjoy it on the return journey.

When he arrived with the single flask, Benedict
thanked him and added gently: "Take care what you find
in the other flask when you go back to pick it up." The
servant, whose name was Exhilaratus, made a hasty exit,
embarrassed and thoroughly bewildered.

Making his way back, he saw the flask in the bushes
exactly where he had left it. Remembering the saint's
warning, he opened it cautiously. It was just as well that
he did, for the wine had run away and inside lay a
poisonous snake. The experience so affected Exhilaratus
that he himself became a monk—a cheery fellow and a
great favorite in the monastery.

Although he turned his back on sinful old Rome and its
worldly excesses, Benedict has nevertheless been called
the last of the great Romans. Into his life as a monk and a
leader of monks he imported the Roman passion for order, discipline and regulation; and in Monte Cassino itself he observed Roman customs which he himself admired.

Under the law of Diocletian, officials of senior rank
were accorded the privilege of having a slave hold a light
for them while they dined. At dinner in the monastery,
Benedict had a monk hold a light for him. Most considered it an honor, but not so one young man. He was well
born, his father was a senior official, and as he stood
there, holding the candelabra, he suddenly felt an inner
surge of anger. Why should a man of his background
perform the function of a slave?

Of course he did not say anything, but immediately
Benedict turned and looked at him sorrowfully.

"What are you saying, my brother?" he asked. "Make
the sign of the cross on your heart!"

Then he ordered the light taken away, and told the youngster to go and get a grip on himself. Once again, there was no penance, no rebuke. None was needed.

Though these and many other miracles are credited to Benedict—he is said to have raised a poor woman's child from the dead—none was an important as the book which he wrote in his tower chamber at Monte Cassino, working far into the night by the light of a guttering candle.

> Let the Brothers fear God and love their abbot, sincere and humble in their affection. Let them prefer nothing whatever to Christ . . .

> Let them put up with one another's weaknesses, whether of body or character, as patiently as possible . . .

> Let no one follow what he thinks is good for himself, but rather what is good for his brother . . .

> Over and above everything, we must take care of the sick: they must be served as though they were Christ Himself . . .

These are some of the words we might have read had we been able to look over his shoulder. Benedict's *Holy Rule* was written primarily for his monks, but it is much more than a set of regulations. It is one of the great spiritual books of all time. Few men have understood human nature so thoroughly as Benedict, and there are few Christians, whatever their situation, who cannot profit from his advice. In the *Rule* he speaks to us as he spoke to the Brothers gathered round him, and his personality comes shining through on every page. Sometimes he is stern, sometimes he has a twinkle in his eye; always he is kind, practical and wise.

In his introduction, he calls the monastery "a school of
the Lord's service" and begs new monks not to be discouraged if any of the rules seem strict. The beginning is
bound to seem hard, but perseverance brings its own
reward. Work, prayer and obedience make the monk love
God more and more, and so he will find strength and
reach the heights.

For the abbot, Benedict has this advice:

> It is his job to serve the brothers rather than to rule
> over them. . . . If he has to discipline anyone, he
> must do it prudently and not be too severe. If he
> scrapes away too hard at the rust he might break the
> vessel! A good abbot wants to be loved rather than
> feared. He must not be too headstrong in his deci-
> sions, but he must not be a worrier either. He must
> not be extravagant or stubborn, jealous or over-
> suspicious.

A newcomer must be genuinely determined to become a monk, and in Benedict's time it was customary to
leave him at the monastery gates for a while, knocking
vainly for admission! If he showed himself a man of spirit
and went on knocking, he had passed the first test. The
gate would eventually be opened and he would be put
into the guest-house for a few days while the Brothers got
to know him.

This frigid treatment was for a special purpose, and
quite untypical of the monastic spirit as a whole. The
ordinary wayfarer or visitor was always assured of a warm
reception at the monastery; in this, as in everything else,
Benedict lays down precise instructions:

> The doorkeeper should always have a cell near the
> gate, so that anyone arriving is always sure of finding

someone on hand to give him a welcome. As soon as
anyone knocks, the doorkeeper must answer *Deo
gratias*, or give him a blessing, and open the gate
quickly.

One problem of those early days were the "monks" who
wandered about the countryside claiming food and shel-
ter wherever they could find it; unstable men with no
real vocation, trading on the habit and the tonsure but in
fact little better than tramps. Surely the door should be
shut smartly on them? Not at all, says Benedict; a wan-
dering monk might have a perfectly genuine reason for
being on the road and he should be made welcome. Furthermore, if he should make any sincere criticism of the
monastery or its Community, he should be listened to
patiently. Who knows, perhaps God has sent him for that
very purpose. But if he should turn out to be merely a
complainer or a troublemaker, then he should be asked
to leave. "And if he be unwilling to go," adds Benedict
darkly, "let two stout brothers explain the matter to
him!"

A supreme administrator, he thought of everything. In
the *Rule* the sublime jostles the mundane in a way that
seems wholly natural, and life at Monte Cassino springs
up vividly before our eyes. On one page we read that in
the monastery the abbot fills the place of Christ, on
another that Brothers sent out on horseback shall be issued with breeches.

Though the abbot rules as a father, he is bound to
consult his monks on important matters, and then even
the youngest Brothers must be allowed their say. What is
more, they must be listened to; for, says Benedict, sometimes God speaks through the young. The elderly and the
middle-aged have no monopoly of wisdom.

Though the monks' diet was certainly frugal, it was

more plentiful than the Egyptian pioneers had enjoyed. In wine-growing countries, says Benedict, they are to be allowed wine at table. "But if it is not available," he adds cheerfully, "the Brothers must not fret over it." Two main dishes should be available, so that a Brother who does not like one may partake of the other. A pound of bread a day is the normal ration, but brothers on heavy work get more at the abbot's discretion. Another important duty for the abbot: he must see that each new Brother gets a habit that fits.

Although prayer, and especially the singing of the Divine Office, was the monks' supreme task, ordinary labor came close behind in importance, since the monastery had to be self-supporting and the work was itself a form of prayer; something daily offered to God. Whatever the monks did, therefore, they did supremely well because they put heart and soul into it. They turned marshes into fertile farmland; they built such magnificent churches as London's Westminster Abbey; they copied the manuscripts which kept sacred and secular learning alive; they tended the sick and they taught school. The monks, almost alone, kept European culture alive during the Dark Ages.

Later on, as in all human institutions, there was a falling-off from the original ideals. Partly because they had done their work so successfully, monasteries became rich and powerful. But whenever corruption became a real threat, God sent men like St. Bruno and St. Bernard of Clairvaux to call monks back to the ways of St. Benedict. And when persecution came, there were brave men from the monasteries ready to die for the faith just as they had lived for it; men like St. Ambrose Barlow, who in the 17th Century returned to England from his French cloister and, although suffering from tuberculosis, worked underground as a missionary until he was caught and executed.

Benedict's own death was a singularly happy one. At the foot of Monte Cassino lived his sister, Scholastica. She, too, had devoted her life to God, though she does not seem to have been a nun in the formal sense, though Benedict visited her regularly and she enjoyed his spiritual direction.

One day in 547, after they had spent a happy day together, Benedict rose to go.

"Don't leave me, dear brother," pleaded Scholastica urgently. "Stay the night and we can talk more of Heaven."

"But you know I can't do that," he repied, mildly surprised. "My Rule says I have to be back by nightfall—and what I lay down for others I have to obey myself."

Scholastica did not reply. Instead, she bowed her head in prayer. Benedict was bewildered; she looked so grave and sad that he wondered what could be wrong. Suddenly there was a clap of thunder and the rain burst in torrents over the mountain and the valley. There was no going back in *that* downpour!

Scholastica raised her head and smiled. With God's help, she had got her way. The thunderstorm had been an answer to her prayer.

Three days later, Scholastica died. There was no warning; she had been in good health. But she had known that her end was near. Benedict had her body brought to the abbey for burial. A few months later, he joined her in Heaven.

A postulant arriving at a Benedictine monastery today will not find the door shut in his face; in all probability, he will be welcomed at the bus station by a young monk driving the monastery car. Benedict would wholly approve, for he knew as well as anyone that 14 centuries would inevitably bring their changes.

Yet a would-be monk has to test his vocation, and he still tests it against the Rule which Benedict wrote in his tower cell so long ago. It remains the essential guide-book for monks and nuns all over the world—and a constant inspiration to many lay people also.

God's Consul

Most people know the story of St. Gregory the Great and the slave-boys. Leaving aside St. Peter and the New Testament account, it is probably the best-known tale ever to involve a Pope.

Gregory, at that time a monk, was walking through the market-place in Rome one day when he saw some fair-haired youngsters on offer at the stand of a local slave-master. On inquiring where they came from, he was told that they were Angles.

"A good name, too" the future Pope replied. "They look like angels. And they ought to be co-heirs with the angels in Heaven."

He resolved then and there that he personally would go as a missionary to the heathen English. But his election as Pope intervened. He sent instead a fellow-monk named Augustine, who succeeded in converting the people of Kent after some minor setbacks caused chiefly by his own tactlessness.

Although some dismal scholars have suggested that the encounter in the slave market never happened, or that the Angles were only tourists, most of us will prefer to go on believing the story just as it has always been told. That Gregory *did* send Augustine and that a lot of English were converted is denied by nobody.

Had Gregory achieved nothing else he would deserve to be remembered, but in fact he was one of the most remarkable men ever to be elected Pope. Though Benedict is sometimes called the last of the great Romans, he was not quite the last. That title rightfully belongs to Gregory.

Few families can say that they have given three popes to the Church, but Gregory's family did just that. Agapitus I and Felix III were both, like Gregory, called Gordianus. Felix, a widower, was actually the saint's great-great-grandfather!

The Gordianus clan were one of the very last patrician families remaining in Rome when Gregory was born, around the year 540. For by this time, the Eternal City was no longer the capital. The Emperor ruled from Constantinople and the western half of the Empire was in charge of an Exarch based in Ravenna. To Ravenna or Constantinople, therefore, most of the great families had gone.

The city they left behind was largely in ruins, for little rebuilding had been done since the barbarian invasions a century before. There was not even a proper water supply; nobody had mended the aqueducts.

It was not a cheerful setting for a youngster to grow up in, and for Gregory, especially, boyhood was a gloomy and a lonely time. His father, whom he dearly loved, died young; his mother promptly retired from the world to live in a nun's cell, leaving Gregory in the hands of tutors.

They taught him grammar and dialectics, at which he did not shine, although he became a brilliant lawyer. They taught him rhetoric, at which he excelled. His education complete, he followed his father's footsteps into the civil service. There, his energy and intelligence won him such rapid promotion that at little more than 30, he was appointed Prefect of Rome.

Though the city itself was in a sorry state, the position of Prefect was still a powerful one. When the Prefect went out, he rode in a chariot drawn by four horses and wore the purple cloak of the emperors. And indeed, Gregory looked every inch an emperor, with his lofty forehead, dark eyes, strong mouth and fine jaw. When he spoke his delicate fingers carved the air to emphasize his words.

His territory included, not only the city itself, but a large part of Southern Italy, down to and including Sicily. Over this vast area, he ran the whole economy. He organized grain supplies and administered poor relief. He supervised whatever building work was done. Baths, sewers, river-banks—all these came under his scrutiny.

Gregory was a successful Prefect. He had drive and endless energy; he got things done. Yet success brought him no real happiness. Looking out over ruined Rome, he found a matching emptiness within himself.

He had read St. Benedict's Rule and the conviction grew steadily that he ought to become a monk. He did not make any hasty decision; for a time, as he himself tells us, he was pulled between the world and the monastery. In the end, the monastery won. At the age of 34 he divided up his inheritance; some he gave to the poor and some he used to endow six monasteries in Sicily. With the rest, he converted the family palace on the Caelian Hill into a monastery, dedicated it to St. Andrew, and became a monk in his own home.

He did not begin his monastic career as an abbot; instead he put the monastery in the charge of Valentius, a holy and experienced man. The former Prefect, who had ridden about in purple, now wore a simple habit and obeyed like the humblest of his brethren.

Whether Valentius was over-awed by the distinguished novice we do not know, but it seems that he failed to curb Gregory's excessive enthusiasm for fasting and night vigils. As a result, Gregory began to suffer from chronic indigestion and heart trouble—two ailments that plagued him for the rest of his life.

Despite this he always said that his three years as a simple monk were the happiest he ever spent. He lived almost entirely on vegetable roots which his mother sent to him on a silver dish, the last of the family heirlooms. One day, he gave the dish away to a shipwrecked sailor begging in the street. According to tradition, he then saw a vision of the sailor, as an angel, handing him the dish back. At the time Gregory had no idea what the vision meant.

It was a new pope, Pelagius II, who brought Gregory's monastic career to an abrupt halt. Fewer popes have been faced with more urgent problems. Floods had swept through the city, days of torrential rain which turned the streets into canals and drove hundreds from their homes. When the waters fell, plague germs bred from the mud and filth killed many of the population. To crown it all, the Lombard invaders were pushing from the north, nearer and nearer to Rome. Most people, including Gregory, were convinced that the world was coming to an end.

In the middle of the crisis, Pope Benedict died and Pelagius succeeded. He came to a swift decision. At a time like this, the most able man in Rome had no place behind monastery walls! To his surprise and alarm, Gregory found himself bound for Constantinople.

His mission was to persuade the Emperor Tiberius to send Rome the help it so desperately needed. Tiberius was a religious man, but he seemed reluctant to act and Gregory's repeated petitions failed to galvanize him. Then Tiberius died and was succeeded by a bandy-legged little general called Maurice, who was not religious at all. After seven unhappy years, Gregory was recalled to Rome.

Gratefully, he retreated once more to his monastery on the hill. The Byzantine capital, with its endless intrigues, had disgusted him. The unfamiliar babble of Greek had made him feel intensely alien; apparently, he never attempted to learn it. This time he was left in peace for five years.

The interruption, when it came, was even more swift and dramatic than before. In the year 590, Rome was again hit by floods and by plague. In the middle of the disaster, just as his predecessor had done, Pope Pelagius died. Soon the cry was going round Rome, first a rumble and then a roar. Gregory for Pope!

To say that Gregory was horrified would be putting it much too mildly. Gregory for Pope? Why, he did not even intend to become a priest! Hurriedly, he wrote Emperor Maurice begging to be excused the honor. He was, he pleaded, a recluse by nature, not at all the sort of public figure needed for the papal office. His letter never reached Constantinople. Germanus, Gregory's successor as Prefect, intercepted it and substituted another, asking that Gregory be elected.

St. Paul had used a basket to escape death in Damascus. Gregory used the same mode of transport to flee from the Throne of Peter. For three days after his friends had smuggled him out, the people of Rome fasted and prayed that God would winkle him from his hiding-place. On the third day, it is said, a divine spotlight shone from Heaven on the spot where Gregory was lying low. Now it was all up. Gregory, virtually a prisoner, was carried back to the city. On September 3, 590, he became Pope Gregory.

He was now 50 years old. Since his return from the East, he had become abbot of his monastery. Into his new home he took some of the monks from St. Andrew's. "God allows me to have them here," he wrote, "as a sort of sheet-anchor. By their example, they keep me fastened to the peaceful shore of prayer whenever I am tossed about by the endless waves of worldly affairs."

The image of the frail rowing-boat scarcely fits Gregory. To our eyes, he looks much more like a huge aircraft carrier, ploughing confidently through every storm. Nobody had fought harder to avoid becoming Pope, yet once he saw that it was useless, he tackled his new responsibilities as though he had been waiting all his life for the chance.

His first act was to proclaim three days of prayer to beseech God's help against the plague. While poor victims collapsed in the streets, seven great processions wended their way from Roman churches to the Basilica of St. Mary Major. Throughout the time Gregory preached and encouraged, and on the third day, the plague began to abate. According to an old legend, St. Michael was seen, at the top of Hadrian's tomb, sheathing his sword. To commemorate the deliverance, a figure of the archangel was placed over the tomb, where it still stands, and the building became known as the Castel Sant Angelo, which name it still has.

Gregory quickly realized that if he was to be a good Pope, he would have to take over many of the duties that really belonged to the Emperor. Nobody knew better than he that the ruler in far-off Constantinople did not really care very much about Rome or Italy, although he continued to extort money from them. Even the Exarch, his so-called deputy, rarely came down from Ravenna to visit the one-time capital.

Soon the people no longer turned for help to the Emperor, or the Exarch, or even to the Prefect. They turned to Gregory, the Pope.

His first concern was for the poor, of whom there were vast numbers. Fortunately the Church owned great estates—the so-called Patrimony of Peter—which stretched from Tuscany down to Sicily. These Gregory set himself to reorganize, to make more profitable, so that the money could be used for relief.

All the skill and experience which he had gained as Prefect now went to the service of the Church. Had he lived today, it would be easy to imagine him at the head of a multinational corporation, for his grasp of detail was total and his business sense acute.

"Cows which have become old and sterile and bulls which are useless must be sold," he wrote Sicily, "in order that at least the price they bring may be used profitably. We will also get rid of those herds of mares which we have been hanging on to, but we will keep 400 foals for breeding. We cannot go on paying the herdsmen 600 *solidi* when we do not get 60 pennies from their animals."

Like a modern accountant, he reveled in figures and balance-sheets. Any subordinate called to his office knew that he had better have done his homework.

Yet he never forgot for a moment why he was so immersed in worldly business, and he knew how to give charity in such a way as to make the recipient feel that he was honoring the Pope in accepting it. When a monastery in Catania was in financial trouble, he wrote the abbot:

"You should not have been ashamed to tell me that you were in need. These funds that I handle don't belong to me, they belong to the poor. I am only the steward who looks after them. It really was very wrong of you not to confide in me . . . I am putting you down for an annual allowance of ten *solidi* from the Sicilian estates. Please accept this, not as a gift from Gregory, but as a blessing from St. Peter."

The thought that his real function was to serve rather than to rule possessed him completely. To an over-effusive lady he wrote: "There is no need to keep on

calling yourself my handmaiden . . . As Pope I am the
servant of the servants of God." Every pontiff since Gregory has claimed the same title. When he heard that a
poor man had died of starvation, he held himself personally responsible. He did severe penance and refused to
say Mass for several days.

It was in 593, when he had been in office for a mere
three years, that Gregory performed his mightiest service
to the Roman people. Several times already the wild
Lombards from the North had pushed their way towards
the city; each time, they had been held back. Now they
were on the march again and this time, it seemed clear,
there was to be no stopping them.

Nearly a century and a half before, another Pope, Leo
the Great, had gone out unarmed to meet Attila the Hun
when he, too, had threatened Rome. Attila, his forces
weakened by disease, had withdrawn without attacking.

Legend says that the whole scene was repeated: Gregory and the Lombard king, Agilulf, met eyeball-to-
eyeball on the steps of St. Peter's; and Gregory, by force
of personality, compelled Agilulf to back down.

The truth is almost certainly less dramatic. It is doubt-
ful whether the two men ever actually met. Nevertheless,
Agilulf *did* back down and Gregory was responsible. He
organized the city's defenses so successfully that the
Lombards knew they might easily be thrown back if they
attacked.

What was more, the Pope encouraged Catholics
throughout Italy to stand up to the would-be invaders.
Nobody, said Gregory, must refuse his military duty on
grounds of religion.

So when the Lombards did arrive outside Rome, they
knew that they were facing a tough opponent. They had
other problems as well. They were threatened by disease,
just as the Huns had been, and Agilulf had left some

highly untrustworthy subordinates behind in the North: men who might easily try to steal his throne while he was away.

All these were good reasons for not attacking the city. On the other hand, the Lombard king could hardly draw back, for that would involve a grave loss of face.

"If I had wanted to lend myself to the destruction of the Lombards," said Gregory later, "they would now have neither king nor dukes nor counts—we could have left the whole nation in a sorry state. But, fearing God, I chose not to take part in destroying anyone."

Revealing words! They show that, despite himself, Gregory was still a proud Roman. He would dearly have loved to give these barbarians a hiding. But a Pope has to be a man of peace, so Gregory arranged a compromise. In return for being left alone, the Romans would pay an annual cash tribute. Agilulf retired with his honor intact.

Who were these Lombards, who constantly terrorized Italy? Centuries before, they had come from Germany to settle in the north of the country. Converted to the Arian heresy, they still practised it, although Agilulf had married a Catholic queen from Bavaria.

In the end, with this lady's help, Gregory was able to arrange a more permanent peace for the whole of the country, and the Lombards themselves became Catholics.

Like Augustine of Hippo, Gregory felt keenly the pressure of his day-to-day duties. Like Augustine, he nevertheless produced an astonishing volume of sermons, books and letters. Unlike Augustine, he never saw himself as an intellectual but as a simple pastor. And even that role, as we know, he accepted unwillingly. He had little time for the flowery or the ornate; his Latin style is lucid, simple and direct. No one ever accused him, as they accused Paul, of preaching above the heads of his congregation. Nevertheless, his psychological insight was profound, as profound as his knowledge of Scripture. So he, too, is honored as a Doctor of the Church, the first, incidentally, to formulate clearly the doctrine of Purgatory.

Probably the most successful of all his books was the *Pastoral Rule*, which he wrote in reply to a friend who chided him for not wanting to become Pope.

"No one presumes to teach any art unless he has, with intense preparation, set himself to learn it," Gregory begins. "What could be more rash, then, than for an unskilled man to assume pastoral authority, since the care of souls is the art of arts?"

Yet since he is now Pope, albeit against his will, he must do his best and offer his guidance, such as it is, to his fellow-bishops. His central message is, as we might expect, very simple. Pride and arrogance are the chief enemies of anyone in spiritual authority. Only humility will win men over. Bishops must love—and by that, he means that they must have a genuine affection for people. Sinners must always be treated gently; undue severity only discourages them and makes them sin more.

Some of this advice might seem fairly obvious to us, but it was needed in those days of severe penances and thundering anathemas. The book was a resounding success and remained so for centuries. King Alfred translated it into English, and when Charlemagne became Holy Roman Emperor he directed that every new bishop receive a copy at his consecration.

Gregory's compassion was not limited to his own flock. He sternly rebuked Catholics reported to him for persecuting Jews, and when Sardinian Jews complained that their synagogue in Cagliari had been seized and turned into a church, Gregory ordered that it be returned to them. On another occasion he showed firmness of a different kind—when Augustine and his fellow missionaries got a bad attack of cold feet en route for England. Traveling through warlike Gaul, they began to wonder nervously what dire fate awaited them in the barbarous, unbelieving, fog-shrouded island for which they were headed. Longing for the Italian sunshine and the safety of the monastery, they wrote requesting permission to return. "Better not to have begun than turn back now!" replied Gregory bracingly. Encouraged, they pressed on.

When they arrived, they found their task easier than they had expected, for the Southern English were already in contact with Christians in France, and their king Ethelbert had married a Christian queen.

In missionary terms it was sound strategy to convert this part of Britain, for monks from Ireland and Scotland had already established a flourishing Church in the north of the country. This Celtic Church, lacking contact with Rome, was beginning to show a certain waywardness. As we shall see in the next chapter, the success of Augustine's mission eventually helped to bring it back into line.

At the other end of the Empire, however, Gregory faced a much graver threat to his authority. The Bishop of Constantinople, a formidable ascetic known as John the Faster, had begun to assume disciplinary functions that properly belonged to the Pope. Even more seriously, he had awarded himself the title "Universal Bishop".

The rivalry between Rome and Constantinople was to smolder for centuries, until the Eastern Schism finally brought about the split between Catholics and Orthodox which persists down to the present time.

Gregory, meanwhile, asserted the papal authority forcefully—so forcefully that in the West, at least, it was not seriously questioned again for another thousand years. There was, he declared, only one Universal Bishop— the Bishop of Rome. Constantinople might now be the imperial capital, for what that was worth, but it was to Peter that Our Lord had given the Keys.

"Work as though everything depended on you, pray as though everything depended on God." Nobody in history has lived that injunction quite so completely as Gregory. For amazingly, throughout his entire career, he remained convinced that mankind really was coming to an end. It was the natural reaction of a patrician who had seen, from his home on the Caelian Hill, the ruins of the palace from which the Emperors had once ruled the world. If the Empire was finished, what could be left for humanity? All around him, he saw the fulfillment of Ezechiel's prophecy: "Woe to the bloody city, of which I will make a bonfire. Heap together the bones and I will burn them in a great fire and the flesh shall be consumed." He even wrote a book to prove that this was indeed happening. And yet he worked as though he, Gregory, could prevent it. As a result, he brought a measure of lasting peace to Italy, and he left the papacy strong against the trials to come.

Gregory did so much that perhaps it is not surprising that he has been credited with one or two extra achievements. He did not, it is fairly certain, invent Gregorian chant, nor did he carry out other liturgical reforms attributed to him. Yet what he did accomplish is astonishing indeed.

He had a little weakness—strange in so forceful and so holy a man—for the wild and fanciful. He was apt to believe any highly colored tale so long as it had a pious moral. One of his books, the *Dialogues*, is full of these.

Gregory died on March 12, 604. His tombstone called him "the Great Consul of God." He would certainly have disapproved, but history has endorsed the epitaph.

A Holy Mix-Up

The executioner knew his job: he killed the Archbishop with one deft and terrible stroke. The crowd, gathered silently before the castle, gasped as the gray, dignified head flew from the shoulders and bounced across the scaffold. A few days before, many of them had knelt for the old man's blessing as he passed into the cathedral for Mass. Now they watched, shocked and bewildered, as he died. But nobody protested. Nobody dared.

From their raised bench beside the scaffold, the bearded Frankish nobles stared impassively as the bloody remains were covered with sacking and dumped into a cart. Then their hard, cold, eyes turned to the next victim, a young fellow, only 24.

He showed no trace of fear as he stood there in his shirt, awaiting the headsman's sword. His circular Roman tonsure showed him to be a cleric, but clearly he was not a Frank. His fair hair and complexion told them that.

"Who is this man?" inquired one of them, frowning. "Why has he been sentenced?"

An official stepped forward.

"This is Wilfrid, Sir," he said. "The Archbishop's assistant. When Annemund was condemned, Wilfrid insisted on dying with him."

"Wilfrid? He's an Englishman?"

"That is correct, Sir," the man replied. "He is from the Kingdom of Northumbria."

An Englishman! The nobles looked at each other. Their king was about to marry an English princess; to kill one of her compatriots might bring trouble on their heads.

"Take him away," commanded their leader. "He's pardoned."

Nobody now remembers why St. Annemund, the Archbishop of Lyons, was executed on that September morning in the year 758. All we know is that somehow he had fallen foul of Ebroin, the so-called "Mayor of the Palace"—the all-powerful official who really controlled the Frankish kingdom.

When Ebroin had the holy old man arrested on a trumped-up charge, Wilfred had been eager to share a martyr's crown. Now God had willed otherwise, he headed back home to Northumbria.

It was by accident that he had found himself in Lyons at all. The son of a minor chieftain, he had left home at 13 to escape from a cruel stepmother. As a page boy at the court of King Oswy, he found himself in a peculiar situation. The King and his subjects, having been converted by monks from Ireland and Scotland, belonged to the Celtic Church and followed Celtic customs. But the Queen, Eanfleda, was from Kent; her people had been converted by Augustine and followed the customs of Rome. As a result, while one half of the court was celebrating Easter, the other half was still keeping Lent!

The Queen quickly took to the earnest young page boy: by her kindness, she tried to fill the place of the mother he had lost. Wilfrid, as we have seen, was nothing if not loyal, so it was hardly surprising that in matters ecclesiastical he came down firmly on the side of

Eanfleda and Rome. This early commitment was to shape the whole course of his life.

Realizing that her young friend was drawn to the religious life, the Queen sent him to Lindisfarne, the island monastery off the coast, to study Scripture and to try his vocation.

Life was hard in that windswept cluster of cells—harder than anything St. Benedict ever envisaged. Sleeping on a plank in his rough woolen habit, getting nothing to eat until three in the afternoon, never tasting meat except on major feastdays—one wonders how any growing boy managed to stand it.

Wilfrid not only stood it, he thrived on it; that he had a vocation nobody could doubt. Only one thing marred his complete happiness: the growing conviction that the Celtic customs of his fellow monks were wrong.

As well as celebrating Easter at a different time, the Celts had their own form of tonsure. Instead of shaving the crown, as did other clerics, they drew an imaginary line across the monk's head from ear to ear and shaved off all the hair in front of that. (In Ireland, pagans called the monks "adze-heads"!) The Celts also had their own way of administering Baptism. Though it varied from the Roman method, it was perfectly valid.

The differences, then, were purely disciplinary, yet on both sides men and women of great holiness clung with fierce tenacity to their method of doing things. By the time he left the monastery, at the age of 18, so convinced was Wilfrid that the Roman way was the right way, that he set off for Rome to learn it properly.

Passing through Lyons, he met Archbishop Annemund. The old man took a liking to the young Yorkshireman just as the Queen had done. He offered him a good job and his niece's hand in marriage. But Wilfrid was not to be deflected; he pushed on to Rome.

His studies there completed—his tutor was the Pope's secretary—Wilfrid again called at Lyons and this time stayed for three years, apparently intending to settle permanently. Annemund's death, however, ended his hopes of a career in the Frankish Church.

Back in Northumbria, Wilfrid soon found an enthusiastic supporter in Alcfrid, son of King Oswy, who ruled the southern part of Northumbria as his father's deputy. He asked Wilfrid to instruct him and his people in Rome's traditions. Alcfrid had recently founded a monastery at Ripon, run by Celtic monks from Melrose, in Scotland. Among them, as it happened, was Cuthbert, himself destined to become one of Britain's best-loved saints. Alcfrid requested the Ripon monks to give up their Celtic ways; Cuthbert and several of his colleagues—including the abbot—refused and went back to Scotland. So Wilfrid became Abbot of Ripon and was ordained priest by a Frankish bishop.

His first act was to put the monastery under St. Benedict's Rule, which he had learned abroad. Then he set about what he saw as his major task: converting the Northern part of the kingdom, which Oswy ruled directly, to Roman usage.

Northumbria, stretching from the East coast to the West coast, included most of what is now Northern England and Southern Scotland. If Wilfrid could win all of it, the Roman party would gain substantial ground. The fact that he had no mandate from Rome, and no jurisdiction outside his monastery, troubled him not at all.

Wilfrid's vigorous campaigning resulted in a famous meeting which took place at Whitby, on England's North-east coast, some time in 663 or 664. Present were the two Kings, Oswy and son Alcfrid, and clerics from both parties. The Celts were led by St. Colman, the Bishop of Lindisfarne. On the Roman side Wilfrid,

though by no means the senior in rank, naturally did
most of the talking.

We have a fairly full account of the proceedings. First,
Colman asserted that the Celtic customs had been insti-
tuted in the East by no less a person than St. John the
Evangelist. He could, however, offer little or no evidence to support this rather surprising claim.

Wilfrid, in reply, pointed out that the Celts, inhabitants of Ireland and Scotland, were standing out against
the rest of the world. This nobody could deny. For good
measure, Wilfrid quoted Our Lord's promise to St. Peter:
"Upon this rock I will build my Church, and to thee I
will give the keys of the Kingdom of Heaven."

King Oswy then took a hand. He inquired whether any
such promise had been given to St. Columba, who
brought Christianity from Ireland to Scotland. The Celts
had to admit that indeed, no promise had been given to
him.

"Do you all, on both sides, admit that Our Lord spoke
those words specifically to St. Peter?" the King asked
them.

Everyone nodded assent.

"Then," declared Oswy, "I will not oppose this
Keeper of the gates of Heaven. Rather, I will obey his
commands to the utmost of my power, lest in the end he
shut those gates against me."

Oswy's pronouncement meant victory for Wilfrid.
Northumbria went Roman. From then on, for Anglo-
Saxon Christians the Pope's word was law and the Archbishop of Canterbury, Augustine's successor, was his
mouthpiece. Colman and his friends did not accept the
decision. Instead they went back to Ireland to found a
new monastery of their own, where they maintained
their adze-head tonsure and continued to compute Easter by the method which St. Patrick had taught. Rome,

unlike Wilfrid, did not interfere with them. It judged, correctly, that Celtic customs would eventually die out of their own accord.

Colman's successor as Bishop of Lindisfarne, Tuda, died within a short time, and Alcfrid chose Wilfrid to take his place. What followed had a distinct touch of comedy.

The neighboring bishops, being outside Northumbria, were not affected by the Whitby decision and most of them went right on with their Celtic practices. Wilfrid declared—quite wrongly—that they were in schism. More Roman than the Pope, he refused to accept consecration from their hands and went off to France to seek it from men whose tonsures were round and whose Easter calculations were impeccable.

Something—we know not what—delayed his return, and when he eventually set sail a shipwreck delayed him even further. When he finally did reach Northumbria, he got a big shock.

During his absence a quarrel had broken out between Oswy and Alcfrid. Once again, we do not know the details, but it must have been serious because at this point Alcfrid disappears from history.

Oswy, not wanting his son's protegé as bishop, had appointed a new one, an abbot named Chad, to take his place. When Wilfrid arrived in York, the new seat of the diocese, he found Chad enthroned in his cathedral.

Surprisingly, Wilfrid seems to have taken the reversal quietly. Perhaps there was nothing else he could do. He went back to the monastery at Ripon and functioned as a bishop only occasionally, when he was invited to ordain priests.

In 669 the Pope appointed a new Archbishop of Canterbury. He chose a rather unlikely candidate—Theodore, a monk from St. Paul's city of Tarsus, who had lived for many years in Rome. Even more surprisingly, Theodore, who had never been to Britain in his life, was nearly 70.

Nevertheless, he set briskly about his new duties as Primate of England, and before very long he arrived in York. There, having listened to the story of Chad's consecration, he decided that it was invalid and that Wilfrid was the rightful bishop.

Now Chad might have been expected to protest. He did not. "If you consider that I have not been properly consecrated," he told Theodore, "I willingly resign this charge. I never thought myself worthy of it in the first place: I accepted it only under obedience."

Theodore, deeply impressed, made Chad's consecration valid and appointed him Bishop of Mercia. (Like so many other people in this story, both Chad and Theodore became, in due course, canonized saints.)

So Wilfrid, at last, took over the diocese of York, and a very conscientious bishop he was. However, though he little suspected it, even worse trouble lay ahead. Once again, it was partly of his own making.

King Oswy had now been succeeded by a prince named Egfrid. Egfrid's wife, Etheldreda, had been pushed into marriage for political reasons; she had not wanted to get married at all. At heart she was a nun and she refused to consummate the marriage. She went on refusing for ten years.

Egfrid appealed to Wilfrid, but instead of helping him, Wilfrid helped Etheldreda instead. With the bishop's connivance, she left her husband for a convent.

The marriage was annulled and Egfrid married again. His new Queen, Ermenburg, was not in the least grateful to Wilfrid, even though he had, in a way, created this opportunity for her. Apparently, she did not trust a man who set so much store by virginity! She, even more than

Egfrid, was extremely hostile. She complained to Theodore that Wilfrid's standard of living was scandalously luxurious. In the end, her campaign of slander succeeded. Wilfrid was deposed.

Wilfrid, bent on an appeal, set out for Rome. But the wind drove his ship on to the coast of Friesland, the large island off the Dutch mainland. He was stranded there for months, but the time was not wasted. For the islanders, when he arrived, were pagan. By the time he left, many were Christian.

During his stay in Friesland, his old enemy, Ebroin— the Mayor of the Palace in Lyons—tried to persuade the islanders to give Wilfrid up to him. Evidently, he had decided that Wilfrid was now too powerful to be allowed to live. But he got nowhere. The lords of Friesland sent his emissaries packing.

Reaching Rome at last, Wilfrid succeeded in his appeal; the Pope ordered him reinstated. It did him no good. Egfrid refused to accept the decree, yelling that Wilfrid had used bribery to obtain it. Within hours, Wilfrid found himself in a dungeon, and there he remained for the next nine months.

Once again, this forceful, aggressive man bore his humiliation with extreme meekness. He spent most of the time in prayer, and he is credited with the miraculous cure of his jailer's wife when she became gravely ill.

Released, Wilfrid removed himself to the pagan Kingdom of Sussex, where he not only carried out mass conversions but set up a new fishing industry, teaching the local eel-catchers the more sophisticated methods he had seen along the East coast of Northumbria. He adapted their nets so that soon the men of Sussex were netting herring and mackerel as well as eels.

Old Archbishop Theodore, meanwhile, was dying. He now realized that he had misjudged Wilfrid and he begged his pardon for the wrong he had done him. He even asked Wilfrid to become his successor, but Wilfrid asked only to be restored to his own diocese of York.

He was indeed restored, but not for long! This time he seems to have fallen out with Aldfrid, King Egfrid's successor. Once more, he was banished from York. He found a new home at Lichfield, where he served as Bishop for some years; but the new Archbishop of Canterbury, St. Behrtwald, disapproved of Wilfrid and at Aldfrid's instigation, he called a synod which demanded that Wilfrid resign Lichfield and retire to the monastery at Ripon.

Just as he had done before, Wilfrid appealed to the Pope. Although he was now nearly 70, he again made the long journey to Rome, and again he skilfully out-argued his opponents. Though he won his case, for the sake of peace he did not, this time, stand on his rights. He agreed to live in semi-retirement and let yet another saint, John of Beverley, rule the diocese of York.

Poor Wilfrid! His life had been one long battle to stay on his episcopal throne, while enemies on all sides strove to unseat him. And, even though he won in the end, it was a hollow victory. When he died, on October 12, 709, he was in a monastery far from York. They buried him at Ripon, the town where he had been abbot and where, it is said, he had been born.

Why did so good a man attract so much hostility? He was brave, he was kind, he was devoted to his flock. He cemented Rome's authority when it was, temporarily at least, in question. He was everything a bishop ought to be.

One quality he did lack, though: tact. He tended to put his head down and charge, when a little diplomacy would probably have been much more effective—and would have brought him less trouble! Yorkshire folk have a reputation for bluntness, and Wilfrid had more than his share. Like Jerome, he was a quarrelsome saint; he was always rubbing people up the wrong way. And unfortunately, the people he rubbed were often the ones with the power to do him harm.

Though he provoked hostility, he inspired affection, too, especially among the poor and the humble. The man who laid the law down at Whitby was also the man who taught the Sussex fishermen a better way to catch fish. Kings and bishops may have been overawed by him, but somehow I do not think that children ever were.

A Viking Bold

When they trundled their god out to meet him, Olaf the
King had a hard time keeping his face straight. Though
the idol stared ferociously in the dawn, it was a pretty
ramshackle affair. It had lost some paint from its nose
and one of its arms wobbled. They must have had it for
many years; indeed, it was probably a good deal older
than any of the sweating warriors who now lifted it rever-
ently from its cart and set it down in the center of the
meeting-ground.

As the warriors stepped back, Dale-Gudbrand, their
leader, faced Olaf triumphantly.

"There, King!" he said. "There is our Thor—a god you
can see and touch. A god to whom we nightly offer bread
and meat."

"And does he eat it?" Olaf inquired gravely.

"Of course he eats it!" snapped Dale-Gudbrand. Here
in his own territory, the chieftain reigned supreme. He
had no need to be polite to any King, and certainly not to
this fool whose prayers went to an invisible deity in the
sky. "He eats it," Dale-Gudbrand repeated. "Each night
we put the food there—and each morning it is gone!"

Olaf did not smile. He did not want to spoil the surprise he had planned for them. Besides, he remembered
the days when he, too, had believed in Thor.

He glanced at Eric, standing impassively beside him. Eric knew what to do, but it would not be easy. When the chance came, he would have to move swiftly.

Dale-Gudbrand, noticing their silence, misunderstood it. Oh yes, they looked down in the mouth now! Not so much to say for themselves, now that they had met Thor. Even the mealy-mouthed fellow from England—the so-called bishop—even he was silent in the presence of mighty Thor.

"Well," said Dale-Gudbrand, a sneer curving the corners of his mouth. "What about this god of yours then? Have you asked him for a fine day after all this rain?"

"I have," replied Olaf, evenly. "I have spent a whole night in prayer."

"And got no reply, I'll wager!"

At that moment, the first rays of the sun broke over the mountain-top, touching the horns of Eric's helmet.

"Look!" commanded Olaf, pointing. "There is my God's reply."

For a second, all heads were turned towards the mountain, away from Thor. The moment had come.

Stepping forward, Eric drew his club from his belt and struck heavily at the painted figure. The wood must have been rotten: it caved in at the first blow. Before the pagan Vikings had realized what was happening, their god was a heap of painted firewood at their feet. From the heap, in every direction, mice and rats scattered, and snakes slithered and writhed.

Shouting and screaming in terror, the Vikings made off—some towards their farms, some towards the sea-shore and the boats. Those loathsome animals, surely, were only the first sign of the god's anger. They had to escape before Thor's vengeance wiped them off the earth.

But there was no escape. The horses had gone from the

farms. The boats, holes bored below the water-line, lay half submerged and useless.

Wide-eyed and shaking, the Vikings turned towards Olaf, who strode calmly towards them. He had wanted a captive audience and he had got it.

"I don't know what all this fuss is about," he said. "Can't you see now what your god was made of? Can't you see who was eating the bread and meat?"

He waved towards the gold and silver trinkets with which the statue had been festooned.

"Take those away and give them to your women-folk," he commanded. "Don't waste them on a heap of wood!"

So one more Viking settlement was converted to Christianity, and soon a neat wooden church dominated the village where Thor had reigned supreme.

As he rode away, Olaf gave thanks to God. Even though he was King of Norway, he had had to fight for his confrontation with the mighty Dale-Gudbrand. In the battle he captured the chieftain's son, but instead of killing the boy he sent him back to his father with a summons to a solemn meeting—an offer which Dale-Gudbrand could not refuse. And so the challenge had been thrown down: Christian God versus pagan god.

Olaf Haraldsson scarcely had the sort of early training that prepares a man for life as an apostle of Jesus Christ. He was born, in 995, to a family of small-time chieftains who lived west of the Oslo Fjord. He may possibly have been baptised a Christian but he was certainly raised a pagan. He went on his first raid at the age of 12. From then on, he got the usual Viking "education" of murder, pillage, and rape.

Olaf was an enthusiastic pupil. His father had died violently a few months before he was born and his step-father Sigurd was a minor king. Unusually for a Viking leader, Sigurd was more interested in agriculture than in fighting. The story goes that he once asked young Olaf to saddle his horse. Within a few minutes, the lad appeared leading a goat, saddled and bridled: a fit mount, he declared, for a man of his stepfather's tastes.

At 14, Olaf had already decided that there was little future for him in a Norway ruled partly by Sweden and partly by Denmark, so he sailed south with one of the gangs seeking booty abroad. In the year 1009 he landed on England's South coast with the invading Danish army, and when the English King, Ethelred the Unready, paid off the Danes to gain peace, young Olaf got his share of the *Danegeld*, as the protection-money was called.

He did not leave, however; instead he changed sides and stayed to help Ethelred fight a new Danish invasion; for of course, the huge bribe which they had received simply made the Danes greedy for more. Olaf fought on the English side in a fierce battle near London Bridge. In later years, when he had become Norway's patron saint, the grateful Londoners built a church there and named it after him.

When the Danes won and Ethelred had to flee to France, Olaf went with him. This visit was to be the turning-point in his life, for it was now that he became a Catholic.

What brought about his conversion we would dearly love to know. According to one account, he saw, in a dream, a tall man who told him: "Go back home, for you are to be Norway's King for all time." Perhaps, on the other hand, he had been moved by the heroism with which priests and other devout Christians met death—and Olaf must have seen many of them die.

It is even possible that Olaf had witnessed the martyrdom of St. Alphege, the brave Archbishop who defended

Canterbury for 20 days against the Danes. Olaf himself, at that time, was one of the invaders. When a traitor at last opened the city gates, Alphege refused to let the citizens ransom him. The men of Kent had, he said, suffered enough extortion already. The Danes, drunk and angry, took him prisoner and pelted him with bones from their feast. Then one of them finished him off with a club.

Whatever occasioned Olaf's dramatic change of heart, from this point onwards he was an unswerving champion of the Christian faith. He was either baptized or confirmed by Archbishop Robert of Rouen, and at once he began to plan the conversion of his homeland.

Under the fierce King Olaf I, Christianity had been made the official religion of Norway and many people in the coastal areas forced to submit to Baptism. Inland, the Norwegians remained largely pagan.

The first Olaf, whose surname was Tryggvesson, had died in battle in the year 999, when our Olaf was only four years old. After his death the Danes and the Swedes had moved in, and many of the Norwegians who had been baptized swiftly reverted to paganism. It is likely that young Olaf Haraldsson's family were among these lapsed converts, in which case Olaf would definitely have been baptized as an infant.

In 1016, with a trusted band of fellow-Norwegians, Olaf sailed once more up the Oslo Fjord that he had known so well as a boy. He got a joyful welcome from his family, who must have been astonished when he told them the project that he had come to achieve: the liberation of Norway from the oppressors and its conquest for Jesus. A pretty large ambition for a youngster who was not yet 21!

Yet he never for a moment doubted that he would succeed—and it soon became clear that he had every right to be confident. The chieftains around the fjord, sick of Danish rule, flocked to him. His support grew and grew.

The Danish King, Canute, was away ruling England, so when the big showdown came it was his deputy, Earl Swein, whose longships faced Olaf's off Nesjar. The battle was long and bloody, but the outcome was decisive. For when it was over, Olaf Haraldsson was the unchallenged King of Norway.

Now he could set about his task of spreading the Gospel, and this he did with the aid of the clergy whom he had brought with him, most of them English. Setting up his capital at Trondheim in the North of the country, he made an English priest, Grimkel, its first bishop. From Trondheim he set out on frequent mission-journeys into the pagan interior, accompanied by Bishop Grimkel and a substantial army.

Their technique was simple. First Grimkel would preach a sermon setting out the essential doctrines of the Christian faith; then Olaf would invite the audience to accept Baptism. If they demurred, Olaf would issue a challenge: "If you will not become Christians, let us fight. And let God send victory to the side whom he favors."

If Jerome and Wilfrid were quarrelsome, what can we say about this warrior saint? At Confirmation we are told to be soldiers of Christ. Olaf took the command literally!

It was scarcely the best way to go about evangelizing a nation. Admittedly, though, it was well adapted to the Viking mentality, which saw fighting as a reasonable way of settling most issues. A Viking warrior did not expect to die in bed; to do so was regarded almost as effeminate.

The grafting of Christianity on to this savage culture at times produced strange results. When some of the nobles around Trondheim revolted against him, Olaf did not kill them. Instead he mutilated the ringleaders and outlawed the rest. This was held to be a splendid example of Christian forebearance.

On the other hand, our Viking saint was a man of deep personal humility, and several stories are told about him which illustrate this. On one occasion, some drunken farmers from the countryside came upon a stranger walking quietly outside Trondheim. When he showed no inclination to laugh and joke with them, they gathered round him and kicked up mud to splash his clothes.

The next day, the farmers were surprised to get a summons to the royal palace. Ushered into the throne room, they recognized, to their horror, the man they had insulted the night before. But Olaf showed no trace of anger. "I just wanted to advise you," he said, smiling gently, "to treat strangers more kindly in future."

One Sunday morning, a group of farm folk, coming into the capital for Mass, found the ferry-man missing, leaving them with no way of getting across the river to church. As they sat pondering what to do next a man walking on the opposite bank spotted their plight. Unfastening a large boat, he rowed over and invited them aboard.

Only when they were half-way across did a woman passenger realize the identity of the oarsman. She was about to cry out in surprise, but Olaf hushed her. "A cow for you from the royal farm if you keep my secret," he whispered. "I don't want anyone to know."

Both stories are probably true: Olaf was not imposing physically and, outside his royal setting, would easily have been taken for an ordinary individual. Thickset and of medium height, he had plain features and a red beard. Only his eyes, bright and piercing, were unusual. He was, rather surprisingly, a gifted artist and wood-carver. Once, when he absent-mindedly carved some wood on a Sunday, he burned the chips in his palm as a penance.

For ten years Olaf carried on his aggressive policy of

conversion. He had a tough struggle in Heligoland, where pagans clung grimly to their sacrifices, but in 1020 Heligoland came to heel. Elsewhere he was equally ruthless in stamping out pagan practices among the nominal Christians. Meanwhile, the warrior-apostle was showing himself a skilful politician, building up a ruling class which had Olaf to thank for its privileges.

Yet all the while resentment was growing, waiting only for an opportunity to show itself. Not only did many of his subjects groan under the Christian yoke and long for their comforting pagan customs; they resented the new legal code which Olaf imposed:

> This is the beginning of our law, that we shall bow to the East and ask Holy Christ for peace and good years, that our land may have many people and that we may be loyal to our King. May he be a friend to us and we to him and may God be a friend to us all.

Olaf's code forbade parents to expose unwanted children at birth, it forbade them to force unwilling daughters into marriage. It imposed fasts and—perhaps hardest of all—it forbade blood-feuds and violent acts of revenge. To Vikings who lived by the sword, this indeed seemed an impossible demand.

In 1026, Olaf formed an alliance with the Swedes and with Ulf, one of Canute's earls who had turned traitor. Thanks largely to Ulf's treachery, they fought another successful battle against the Danes. Olaf must have thought now that his throne was certainly safe. Little did he suspect that Canute's agents were campaigning skilfully among the discontented Norwegian lords, handing out bribes and stirring up their latent hostility against the King whom they regarded as a fanatic.

When, two years later, Canute sailed back from England at the head of a largely English force, Norwegians rose up in their thousands—not, this time, to expel the invader, but to help him expel the King.

For Canute it was a walkover; he did not even have to fight a battle. Though himself a Christian—he had made a pilgrimage to Rome—he was willing to let pagans go their own way so long as they gave him their support.

After hiding out for a while in South Norway, Olaf was forced to flee to Russia. There, he learned that some of his most trusted aides had taken bribes from Canute, and were now working on the Danish side. Nevertheless, he refused to feel bitterness; when one of the traitors returned to him, he forgave him at once.

With Canute back in England, Olaf resolved to try to regain his Kingdom. His wife, Astrid, was a Swedish princess, and he turned for help to Sweden. Raising a small army he crossed into Norway and, with incredible courage, marched towards his old capital Trondheim, where he knew that Danish support was strongest. "Face to face the eagles must fight"—so one of Olaf's Norwegian enemies had warned him, as he went over to the Danish side. Now the moment had come.

The final battle took place at Stiklestad, by the Trondheim Fjord, about 40 miles from the city itself. The army which faced Olaf greatly outnumbered his own. It consisted largely of Norwegians who wanted no more of this austere Christian King.

Though Olaf's forces fought long and bravely, the result was never in doubt. As his men fell around him, Olaf at last found himself face to face with Tore Hund, one of the fiercest of the Danish warriors. Tore prepared to strike at the King, but a loyal warrior—the same man who had taken a bribe and then repented—threw himself between them.

"This is how we hunt bears in Denmark," yelled Tore,

as he ran his spear through the warrior. Olaf was wounded by an axe-blow on the knee, and as he supported himself against a boulder, Tore ran him through.

Olaf died on August 31, 1030; we are sure of the date because during the fighting there was an eclipse of the sun. The traditional date, July 29, is wrong, though it is still kept as Olaf's feast-day.

After all was over, Tore Hund went chivalrously to where his enemy's body lay, to arrange it decently and to close the eyes. As soon as he touched the dead King, a severe wound on his own hand was instantly healed. Olaf had worked his first miracle.

Many more followed in the succeeding year. From the spot where his body was first laid there appeared a healing spring. Remarkable cures were reported there.

With the agreement of the Danes the body was removed to Trondheim, where a great cathedral was consecrated to his memory. It is still Norway's national religious shrine, and a huge statue of the saint looks out over the town.

As news of his holiness spread, Olaf's name became a rallying-point for Norwegians. In praying to him they discovered their national identity and threw off the Danish yoke. Five years after Olaf's death his son, Magnus the Good, became King. At last, Norway was united and it was Christian. In death, Olaf had triumphed.

A Much-Maligned Monk

Now we come to another unpopular figure—Bernard of Clairvaux. Unless you happen to be a Cistercian, it is unlikely that Bernard is the first saint that you will look for when you get to Heaven.

Like St. Paul he is widely regarded as a fanatic—always warning, forbidding, cajoling. The reputation has persisted for centuries. Only recently, a well-known Catholic journalist, who ought to have known better, informed his readers that Bernard was a thoroughly unpleasant fellow. And if that is a Catholic pundit's considered opinion, we can scarcely feel shock when the agnostic philosopher Bertrand Russell calls the great monastic reformer a politician and a bigot—and unintelligent to boot!

Surely, if these men are right, Bernard must have been thoroughly disliked by those who came into contact with him? Surely, people must have scattered in all directions whenever this gray-faced monk hove in sight?

The truth is the exact opposite. Of all the colorful individuals who crowd the Middle Ages, Bernard was one of the most popular and compelling. Mothers, it was said, hid their sons when they saw him coming. Wives hid their husbands and girls their boy-friends. Why? Because they were afraid that Bernard would make monks of their menfolk!

Everywhere he went, he drew men to the cloister in swarms. Few were proof against the charm of this Pied Piper in a cowl. On one occasion, a group of young soldiers, on their way to a tournament, called to see this famous Bernard about whom they had heard so much. Bernard talked to them and gave them some beer. Every single one became a monk.

Not only did Bernard lead the Cistercian reform which swept through Europe with miraculous speed. He was the confidant of kings and Popes, and the friend of many humbler men. At the high point of his career, he was probably the most powerful individual alive. And that is the main clue to his unpopularity. Here was a man, severely ascetic in his daily life, fearless in denouncing evil, wielding tremendous influence without ever becoming Pope or even bishop. Surely there must be something sinister about him, something to account for his sway over the minds of so many?

Bernard was born, the son of a Burgundian nobleman, in the year 1090. From babyhood he suffered from severe migraine. When a local wise-woman was brought, with her charms and spells, to cure him, little Bernard responded by driving her from the room.

Though plainly a lad of character, he at first showed no particular religious inclination. At school he developed a talent for poetry, which, it is said, he employed in composing ribald verses.

His conversion seems to have been a slow, undramatic process, brought about largely by the example of his mother Aleph. Her death, when he was 17, affected him deeply. By the time he was 20, Bernard had set his sights on the priesthood.

From the outset, his vocation was severely tested. He

was extremely good-looking and girls pestered him. One brazen little lady, hoping to seduce him, actually climbed naked into his bed. Bernard woke up, saw the girl, and moved over to make room for her. Then he turned on his side and went back to sleep.

His family would not have minded his becoming a monk had he been prepared to enter Cluny or one of the other rich and powerful monasteries which abounded. But when he announced Citeaux as his choice, they could scarcely believe it. This run-down establishment had been founded years before by St. Robert, Abbot of the nearby monastery of Molesmes. Disgusted with the luxurious living of his fellow-monks, he had moved out to Citeaux with a small group who shared his desire to live more strictly. The Holy See stepped in, however, and ordered Robert back to Molesmes, never to return to Citeaux.

In the succeeding years, most of the Citeaux monks died. The present Abbot, an Englishman named Stephen Harding, was living in the ramshackle buildings almost alone. We can imagine how glad he must have felt when, on that April day in 1112, Bernard came knocking at the door.

For he did not come alone. Incredibly, he had brought somewhere around 30 other postulants with him! Four of them were his brothers; the rest were cousins or friends, young noblemen like himself, the gilded youth of the neighborhood. Some were married men whose wives had themselves agreed to become nuns.

How Bernard achieved this miracle has never been explained—for miracle it undoubtedly was. Not only had the shy, determined youngster overcome his family's opposition; he had actually got most of them to share his new life.

No doubt he was soon telling St. Stephen (yes, he was

canonized too!) of a little incident which occurred just as they were leaving the family home at Fontaines for the last time. Nivard, Bernard's youngest brother, was playing outside with other children and Bernard called a farewell to him. "All our lands and property will be yours now, Nivard," he said.

"You mean you are going to have Heaven and I only get earth?" the little boy replied. "I don't call that fair!"

Sure enough Nivard too became a Cistercian as soon as he was old enough—and so, in the end, did Tescelin, their father.

When he was asked, later on, why he had chosen Citeaux, with all its rigors, Bernard replied: "Because my weak character needs a strong medicine." Whether it needed as strong a medicine as Bernard chose to apply is a question that we must now ask.

Stephen Harding was a saint and, what is more, a man of great scholarship and organizing skill. But was he really such a good novice-master? For, during the three years of Bernard's novitiate, he allowed him to undertake penances so severe that they wrecked his health. (Gregory the Great, you may recall, made a similar mistake.)

"He gave his body hardly enough to keep it in the land of the living," wrote a friend. "He thought that a few moments' sleep and a few mouthfuls of food were quite enough. Night vigils were nothing to him, since he scarcely slept anyway."

The net result of this over-enthusiasm was that after a year in the novitiate, Bernard could no longer digest even the little food that he took, and the constant vomiting plagued him for the rest of his life. In his final years, it got so bad that he could no longer take his place in choir—something which must have caused him the greatest distress.

His friend, William of St. Thierry, recalled that Bernard actually found the very thought of food repugnant in the extreme. Eating became a torture to him and it was only the fear of causing his own death that brought him to the table. All of which sounds suspiciously like the condition which doctors now called *anorexia nervosa*.

Although he had had a nobleman's upbringing and was totally unused to manual work, Bernard took great delight in performing the most menial tasks. He dug ditches, chopped wood, fetched and carried for monks who were skilled craftsmen.

Though he made himself permanently ill, his titanic fasts and vigils did bring him one reward: a degree of recollection which would have been the envy of an Indian yogi or a Zen monk.

"His mind was so fixed on God that he did not see even when his eyes were open," William tells us. "Although he was not deaf, if anyone spoke to him about some worldly matter, he simply did not hear. Even after a year in the novitiate he did not know whether the ceiling of the scriptorium was vaulted or not, and although he often visited the church, he thought that there was only one window in the sanctuary. In fact there were three!"

Bernard was never to lose this capacity to shut off the world and to focus his mind on God. Years later, when he was deeply involved in international affairs, he was traveling along the side of Lake Geneva with a group of companions, when one of them called his attention to the beauty of the lake. Raising his head innocently, Bernard inquired: "What lake?"

Perhaps Stephen thought that a spirit like Bernard's should have free rein. We simply do not know. However, he certainly realized that here was a monk of quite exceptional qualities. When, three years after Bernard's arrival, men were needed to found a new monastery at Clairvaux, Stephen chose Bernard to lead them.

Some of the party were surprised to find themselves

under obedience to Bernard. They were older than he was and they had served the Order for much longer. What was even more to the point, they were all physically stronger. Bernard, surely, was too frail to be an abbot! Nevertheless, Bernard was Stephen's choice, so there was really no more to be said. Together they set out for their new home.

The name Clairvaux means "Valley of Light", but there was nothing light about it before the monks arrived. It had been a haunt of robbers and it was known as the Vale of Wormwood. In this unpromising spot, the monks began to build their monastery.

Pioneers expect a tough time, but the first years at Clairvaux were far tougher than anything these monks had ever experienced. Their poverty was extreme. Often their food was stew made with beech leaves, and bread made with barley, millet and vetch. A visting monk once took some of it away with him and showed it round. It was a miracle, everyone agreed, that men who worked so hard could survive on such fare.

Bernard reveled in the austerities, of course, but in time they took their toll. He became seriously ill.

His friend William, arriving on a visit, found the young abbot living in a little hut like the huts built for lepers at crossroads. William asked how he was.

"Fine," said Bernard, with his usual charming smile. "Even though the Bishop has put me in the care of a crazy brute!"

The well-meaning prelate, concerned for Bernard's health, had ordered him to accept treatment from a worthless quack who plied his patient with remedies which William does not name, but which he assures us were pretty horrible.

When he was a child, he had driven out the wise-woman and her charms; yet now that he was an adult, and a leader respected by all, he practised a childlike obedience. He swallowed the remedies for a year, the period which the Bishop had stipulated, then he dismissed the man with thanks and went back to his own regime, living on a little bread and milk with, occasionally, vegetable-water or baby-broth.

Amazingly, he did get over the illness, and from then on his monks noticed a change in him, Though he was still as hard as ever on himself, he was more sympathetic and tolerant of the weaknesses of others. Day and night he prayed standing, and he wore a hair-shirt until he realized that it could be seen under his habit. Doctors marveled that a man so frail could achieve so much.

Soon stories began to spread through the countryside—stories of miracles which the saint had worked. That he was a saint, nobody doubted.

A poor woman traveled for many miles to see him, bringing her child, whose hand and arm were withered and deformed. She met Bernard as he was coming from the fields. Moved, he asked her to put the child down on the ground, while he prayed and made the sign of the Cross over it. Then he asked the mother to call the little one to her. It ran to her and embraced her with both arms. The deformity was gone.

When the monastery was in desperate financial straits, and seemed about to fail, a woman arrived to beg the prayers of the brothers for her husband, who was desperately ill. She brought an offering with her—the amount they needed. "Go back home," Bernard told her. "You will find your husband quite well again." And he was.

When Bernard himself was again gravely ill and in unbearable pain, he sent one of the monks to the chapel to pray for him. As the brother knelt there, Bernard saw Our Lady, with St. Lawrence and St. Benedict, enter his cell. They laid their hands upon him and he was well again.

Bernard, as we have seen, did not initiate the Cistercian reform; that was done by others. But it was his appearance on the scene, just when the whole experiment seemed about to fail, that miraculously reversed its fortunes.

It was Bernard's example and Bernard's reputation that brought men flocking to Clairvaux and to the other abbeys which he founded year by year. They were from every conceivable walk of life. Priests and bishops, noblemen and peasants—they all came eagerly, to dress in rough woolen habits, to eat the most frugal fare, to pray in unheated stone churches and to turn scrubland and swamps into flourishing pastures.

How the French peasant folk stared as these white-robed monks, at once serene and intense, raised their austere, towerless monasteries out of the ground before their eyes! So quickly did they build, it seemed like magic. And there, in the middle of the activity, was Bernard. Smiling, exhorting, directing—he seemed scarcely strong enough to stand, yet he worked steadily on; a mystic with the strength of a lion and the practical common-sense of a master builder.

When they had finished staring, many of the spectators themselves became Cistercians; low birth was no barrier to acceptance, as it was in most other monasteries. The Cistercians were the first order to welcome the serf class into the monastic life, and this new army of lay-brothers played a vital role in its building program.

It was at the opening of a new abbey, at Foigny, that Bernard performed a rather amusing miracle. Making their final preparations for the ceremony, the Brothers were attacked by a plague of flies that threatened to wreck the proceedings. No amount of swatting made any difference. In the end, Bernard told the creatures solemnly. "I hereby excommunicate you!" On the following morning, every single fly lay dead on the floor and the brothers had to use palings to scrape them up.

Barely 15 years after Bernard entered the Order, the Cistercians had built their first monastery in England. By the time he died, there were 338 foundations, stretching from Sweden to the Middle East. Citeaux, which had once seemed certain to fold up, now had 700 Brothers. Like the Benedictines before them, the new White Monks made an enormous impact on Europe's economy, transforming farming techniques by their skill and hard work.

Unlike the Benedictines, whose abbeys were completely independent of each other, the Cistercians had a strong, centralized organization, with regular visitations to ensure that the Rule was being properly kept. Their monasteries, bare and simple, were built on a common plan, so that one looked much like another.

As the buildings were simple, so were the monks' lives. Mass and the Divine Office were celebrated with as little ceremony as possible, and the churches were bare of ornament. Whenever he saw signs of luxury in a monastery, Bernard waxed vehement. Here is his attack on monkish gluttons:

> At each meal, dish follows dish . . . you get two enormous helpings of fish, your palates are tickled with different sauces, and Heaven knows how many different ways you have your eggs done—soft, hard, minced, fried, baked, stuffed . . . As to water, am I allowed to mention it, since you no longer add it to your wine? Three or four times during the meal you get half-filled goblets to taste. You sniff, you sip— and you always choose the best!

In writing like this, Bernard was bound to make himself unpopular, especially among those whom the cowl fitted! He and his monks were soon accused of pharisaism by the men whose consciences he so rudely pricked. "Oh Pharisees, your descendants are among us," wrote one outraged abbot. "Are you animated by humility when you continually disparage others and praise yourselves?"

Yet Bernard went right on hitting out. Nobody was safe. Monks, secular priests, even bishops—all came under his flailing pen.

What angered him most was their callous indifference to the poor who stood starving at the gates of church or monastery, while those within continued to enjoy their fine food and their riches. It was for the poor that he spoke, as he himself pointed out:

> If I dare to protest against these abuses, I am told that I, as a mere monk, have no right to sit in judgment on bishops. But even if I remain silent, do you think no one else is going to cry out? The naked, the cold, the hungry—you will hear them saying: "Tell us, priests, why do you have all this gold on your horses' bridles? We are starving. The bitter weather eats into our bones . . . Yet you are spending on luxuries money that should keep us, your brothers, alive!"

As one of his modern biographers has pointed out, today's socialist leaders have nothing on Bernard!

The rich ornaments which festooned monasteries and churches annoyed him, not only because they were an insult to the poor, but also because he felt that they distracted monks from their first and most important job— prayer. With typical verve, he demanded:

> What do they mean, these vile and monstrous gargoyles in the cloisters? Why put there hideous apes,

fierce lions, centaurs and hideous creatures that are half-man and half-beast? Why these monsters with several bodies to one head, or with one body and many heads? One animal has a serpent's tail, another is half-beast, half-fish . . . There are so many of these images—some of very real charm—that the monk must be tempted to spend his time admiring them instead of meditating on the word of God!

Here, I think, Bernard overreaches himself. He describes all those weird and wonderful creatures so well that he makes us want to see them! Some of them are charming; he himself admits it. Had everyone listened to Bernard, European architecture would be much the poorer.

Nevertheless, so great was his influence that he was inevitably drawn into the turmoil of the times. For, once again, the Church of God was in an unholy mess.

Not for the first time and not for the last, a squabble had broken out over the Throne of Peter. Pope Honorius II having died, a minority of cardinals hastily elected Cardinal Gregorio Papereschi, a man of honorable life, as Pope Innocent II. The haste was because they feared that the powerful and ambitious Cardinal Pietro Pierleone would try to seize the papacy for himself. They were right. Despite Papareschi's election, Pierleone got a majority of cardinals to back him. There was a second so-called election and Pierleone had himself crowned Anacletus II.

The King of France called a council at Etampes to decide French policy, and insisted that Bernard be present. Bernard came down firmly for Pope Innocent, which assured him of French support, and arranged a meeting at Chartres between Innocent and King Henry I of England. With the help of St. Norbert, German support was recruited too and in the end, Anacletus was routed—but only after a long, hard struggle.

In 1145 Bernard saw one of his own Cistercian monks, Bernardo Paganelli, elected as Pope Eugene III. Bernard did not hesitate to give him some sound advice. He wrote the new Pope:

> There is something I dread for you more than any sword or poison. It is the lust for power. Why have you been set above men? Not to rule over them, I am sure of that! A burden of service is our lot, not the privilege of power.

It was at Eugene's request that Bernard preached the Second Crusade after Edessa, capital of the first Crusader State, had fallen to the Turks. It has been suggested that Bernard was not heart and soul behind the crusade, and that he preached it purely as a matter of obedience. Whether or not that is true, he certainly put much fire into his sermons, inspiring many knights and at least one King, Germany's Conrad III, to set sail. It was all wasted effort. The greed and jealousy of the various Christian factions brought failure on the whole enterprise.

As his own campaign was in full swing, Bernard heard to his horror that a medieval Hitler named Raoul was urging the people of the Rhineland to start their Crusade off by massacring the local Jews. Bernard sent a strong letter to the Archbishop of Mainz denouncing anti-Semitism as a "foul heresy". To the local population he wrote: "For us the Jews are Scripture's living words, because they remind us of what Our Lord suffered. They are not to be persecuted, killed or even put to flight." According to a Jewish writer of the time, Bernard's action saved all their lives.

Compassion was undoubtedly the strongest element in

Bernard's nature. Pied Piper he may have been, but he could still feel for parents who saw their dearly loved son disappear behind monastery walls. To the parents of one boy, who were worried about his health, Bernard wrote:

Do not be sad about Geoffrey, or weep for him. He is going swiftly to joy, not to sorrow. I will be father, mother, brother and sister to him. I will make the crooked paths straight and the rough places smooth. I will organize things so that his soul will advance but his health will not suffer.

Even his opponents could not hate him and did not wish to. There was, inevitably, much tension between the Cistercians and the rich and powerful monks of Cluny, whose abbey church was then the largest church building anywhere in the world. Yet what did Cluny's abbot, Peter the Venerable, think of Bernard? He said that Bernard had been "chosen by Providence as the massive pillar, not just of the entire monastic order, but of the entire Latin Church."

He had a famous controversy with Peter Abelard, which ended with Abelard's doctrinal errors being condemned by Rome. But before moving against him, Bernard saw Abelard privately, argued each point with him, and begged him to retract. Had Abelard done so, he would have saved himself a lot of trouble.

Bernard felt keenly the pressures of the world and longed only to be within his monastery, talking to his monks of the love of God. Yet he had to deal with yet another anti-pope—the so-called Victor IV—and was several times called in to quell civil unrest.

In his spiritual writing, especially in his *Sermons on the Song of Songs*, he traces the long road which a soul must travel on the road to union with God. Yet at the same time, he taught, God is always near and always waiting for us to approach. "Mighty is the Lord and greatly to be feared; little is the Lord and greatly to be loved." He had a great devotion to the Infant Christ and to the Virgin Mary.

Bernard died at Clairvaux on August 20th, 1153, and was canonized a mere 21 years later. In 1830, he was proclaimed a Doctor of the Church.

The Hound of
the Lord

In the year 1204 a Spanish bishop named Diego
d'Azevedo was sent by the King of Castile on a romantic
mission. He was to travel to Denmark to arrange a marriage for the King's son.

The mission ended sadly: the Danish princess died
before the wedding could take place. But for Bishop
Diego and the friend who traveled with him, the journey
was an experience that drastically altered their lives.

The bishop's companion, Dominic Guzman, was 35
when they set out on a trek that took them from one end of
Europe to the other. Dominic, a canon of Diego's cathedral at Osma, had lived a sheltered life. He knew only the
church as it existed in Spain. Spanish Catholics, living
under the threat of Moslem rule, clung fiercely to their
religion.

As soon as they crossed the Pyrenees, the two men
sensed that here it was different—that something was
terribly wrong. In town after town, village after village,
their clerical habit brought no respectful greeting. Men
and women scowled and turned away. Sometimes children mocked them.

Dominic and Diego looked at one another. No need to
ask what explained this sinister behavior.

"Albigensians," said the bishop. Dominic nodded.

Southern France was by now largely in the grip of this strange new creed, with its own sacraments, its own bishops and priests, its own church councils—even its own "pope"! Great lords supported it, but its main strength lay with the common people, who had abandoned the Catholic Church by the thousands, leaving the children unbaptized, the dying without the last rites, and the priests to say Sunday Mass alone.

When they reached the lodging-house in Toulouse, Dominic and the bishop found that their landlord, too, was an Albigensian. As the man leaned forward across the table, eager to recruit these Spaniards to the new faith, Dominic marveled that its bleak doctrines could have found so much favor.

"You fellows have got it all wrong when you talk about Almighty God," proclaimed the landlord. "How can God be almighty when there is so much evil in the world? I'm telling you, the world doesn't belong to God at all, it belongs to Satan. All of it!"

Only the spiritual was in God's domain, he insisted, and a man could only be saved by becoming perfect—by practising a fierce asceticism which cut him away from the material world as much as was possible.

Was their host one of the perfect?

"Ah, no," the man replied, "but I shall be! When I am dying I shall receive what we call the *consolamentum*, then I'll be one of the perfect, just as though I had fasted and stayed celibate. Meanwhile, I shall go right on enjoying life!"

The landlord ended his apologia with a broad wink and leaned back to study its effect.

Now it was Dominic's turn. Patiently, skilfully, he dissected the man's arguments, exposing them for the farrago of nonsense which they were.

In one sense it was an unfair contest. After all,
Dominic had a trained mind. Back home in Osma, as
Diego well knew, his favorite canon was always studying
and when he was not doing that he was praying. Hours
and hours he spent on his knees in the cathedral, sometimes weeping for other men's sins.

All the same, Dominic had no easy task. Dawn was
coming through the casement by the time the landlord,
head in hands, conceded that he had been wrong and
that he must return to the Catholic faith.

If you read the chapter on St. Augustine, you will have
recognized the landlord's Albigensian heresy as the one
which Augustine of Hippo knew as Manichaeism. After
six centuries, it had appeared once again in a new and
more virulent form, not only in France but in several
other countries also. This time, however, there was nothing secret about it. This time the challenge was direct.

Why did the Albigensians win so much ground? One
reason was painfully obvious. Despite all Bernard of
Clairvaux's strictures, despite the Cistercian reform, the
lives of the clergy had improved little if at all. Too many
priests still wallowed in luxury, stuffing themselves with
fine foods while the poor starved at their gates.

Incredibly, the Cistercians themselves were now frequently guilty of those very sins which Bernard had cas-
tigated in others. As Cistercian monasteries got rich and
powerful, Cistercian monks grew sleek and fat.

Despite this deterioration, the Pope asked the Cistercians to preach against the Albigensians. It was a big
mistake. In the first place, few of the monks knew how to
preach, since it was not normally something that they
did. Secondly, their riches made them a laughing-stock.
As the monks rode out on their fine horses, the heretics
pointed to their own "perfect"—the elect few who fasted
and prayed and led lives of superhuman austerity.

Not that the Albigensian heresy was purely a protest against lazy and indifferent clerics. It was, as Augustine had found, very convenient to belong to a religion that allowed you to sin with a clear conscience. For if all matter was evil, so were all human actions, marriage included; therefore it was meaningless to try to be good. The one wholly virtuous act, which few performed, was suicide.

By the time their Danish assignment was over, Dominic and Diego knew that they could not go back to a peaceful life in Osma. Fired with missionary zeal, they went to Rome and sought an audience with Pope Innocent III. Would he please let Diego resign his diocese and could they both go to Russia and convert the Cuman Tartars?

It seemed an odd request. Certainly Pope Innocent thought so. Kindly, he pointed out what should have been obvious.

"My sons," he said. "You have a mission-field much closer at hand. Go instead to the Albigensians!"

The Cistercians were still fighting the heresy in France, but by now their morale was low. The two Spaniards, with their blazing enthusiasm, quickly revived it. More monks were sent in, and soon 40 missionaries were hard at work.

Though Diego was the bishop, Dominic was the leader. Penance and self-denial were his weapons; he preached with his body as well as with his tongue. "A man rules his passions is master of the world," he often declared. "It is better to be the hammer than the anvil."

So he lived for long periods on bread and water, never taking anything more than soup or a couple of eggs. He slept always on the ground, usually in a church, fully dressed and never using a blanket even on the coldest nights, He regularly had himself flogged with iron chains.

He made sure that the heretics knew about his mortifications—not to gain honor for himself, but to show them that the so-called "perfect" were not the only men capable of heroic asceticism.

He was fearless in the face of hostility, so much so that the heretics themselves marveled at it.

"Aren't you afraid that we'll attack you?" asked one peasant in an Albigensian village. "What would you do if we seized you now?"

"Ask you to put me to death as slowly and as painfully as possible," replied Dominic, smiling. "Then my place in Heaven would be all the greater."

I have so far said little of Dominic's early life because little is known. Born at Calaruega in 1170, he got his early education from an uncle who was a priest, then spent ten years at the University of Palencia. While he was still a student Diego asked him to become a cathedral canon, living in Community under St. Augustine's Rule, which he was later to adapt for his new order.

Though deeply studious, when famine struck the district he sold his dearly-loved books and gave the money to the poor.

"I cannot study from dead skins when all around me men in living skins are starving," he declared.

Despite all Dominic's fervor, despite all his self-denial, his monkish companions soon began to feel discouraged again. True, there had been conversions at first and everything had seemed promising. But now they were once more ploughing stony ground.

At the end of 1207 the monks went home and Diego, who had himself become a Cistercian, went home to Spain to get reinforcements. He never came back.

Scarcely had news of his death reached Dominic than fresh disaster struck. Peter of Castelnau, one of the papal legates whom Innocent had sent to organize the struggle, was assassinated. It was the signal for a Crusade.

For about six years the fighting raged, Catholic lords against heretic lords. Popular legend has Dominic marching ahead of the Catholic forces waving a crucifix.

In fact he took no part in the war. Deeply saddened, he preached wherever he could and established a convent at Prouille. Why a convent? Experience among the heretics had taught him that women were doing much of the damage: children were imbibing Albigensian doctrines at their mothers' knee. Dominic wanted a trained force of teachers and missionaries to counteract their influence. Some of his nuns were well fitted to do so, for they themselves had once been heretics.

Peace came in 1215 and Dominic was again able to resume regular missionary work, moving round Toulouse diocese with a small group of companions.

Fulk, the Bishop of Toulouse, was a good friend to Dominic now and later, but the two did not always see eye to eye. In earlier life Fulk had been a troubador, and his taste for showbusiness had not entirely been subdued. When he went on visitations accompanied by soldiers, servants and mules, Dominic had to tell him that prayer and humility were more fitting companions for a bishop.

Three times Dominic was himself offered a bishopric and three times he refused. He had another, much bigger task ahead.

Strangely, it was a group of heretics who led him towards his lifework. Not the Albigensians, of course, but another sect, known as the Waldenses. Their founder, a layman from Lyons, had much in common with Dominic. Revolted by clerical luxury, he called for a return to the poverty of the Apostles. Also, he wanted to preach.

At first the new group won papal approval. The poverty was fine, said the Pope, but not the preaching. They must not do that because they were not qualified. However, the Waldenses went right on preaching in defiance of the ban. Soon they were denying Purgatory and several of the sacraments. Excommunication followed swiftly.

Dominic had a lot of sympathy with the Waldenses, many of whom became Protestants at the Reformation. He spent much time reasoning with them, for he realized that they were trying to fill, however ineptly, a gap that existed in the Church—the gap between clergy and laity.

Now Dominic began to think of a new kind of religious Order that would do just that. An Order that would live in the world and not behind monastery walls. Its members would be mobile, ready to go wherever they were needed. They would be poor and seen to be poor: they would beg in the streets for their bread. Above all they would preach—on village greens, in market squares; anywhere men would listen.

When he traveled to Rome with Fulk in 1214, Dominic must have expected opposition, and he got it. Consecrated beggars were a highly suspect idea. Monks who were not monks, who wandered through the countryside like vagrants, begging instead of working with their hands like the Benedictines and Cistercians—it did nor sound right! Wise old cardinals shook their heads. It looked for a time as though the new Order might be stillborn.

In the end, Pope Innocent over-ruled the objectors. It is said he had a dream in which he saw Dominic support with his shoulder a Lateran Basilica which was about to collapse. He told Dominic to go ahead.

At this time, Dominic had 16 companions. Eight were Frenchmen, seven Spaniards and one, Brother Lawrence, an Englishman. It was now, in August, 1216, that they drew up their first Rule, based on the rule of St.

Augustine but with some added regulations to meet their own needs.

They would sing Office in choir, just as the religious had always done, but their mission-work must come first. If choir clashed with a brother's study or preaching, he was excused choir.

The brothers—or friars—would need houses to live in, but apart from that they would own no property. Later, when a benefactor gave Dominic an estate, he ripped the deed in two. Again, when he thought that a new friary in Bologna looked too palatial, he ordered the work stopped.

The year 1216 found Dominic once more in Rome. Innocent had died but his successor, Honorius III, formally confirmed his new Order of preachers, "in consideration that your brethren will be champions of the faith and a true light of the world."

Here, too, Dominic had a dream—a strange dream in which God seemed about to punish a sinful world but was dissuaded by Our Lady, who pointed out two men to Him. One of them Dominic recognized as himself; the other was a stranger.

Next day, as he was praying in church, a ragged beggar came in. Dominic at once recognized him as the man in the dream. Embracing him, Dominic declared: "If we two hold together, no one on earth can stand against us."

His new friend was Francis of Assisi, and Dominicans and Franciscans have been friends ever since. Each year, on their founders' feast-days, members of the two Orders visit each others' churches to say Mass and to dine together afterwards.

Everyone thought that the new Order of preachers would stay right on working in Toulouse, where Fulk had given it a house and a church, and where heresy was once more gaining ground. There was consternation, therefore, when Dominic dispersed his men, sending some to Spain and some to Paris. Only four remained in Toulouse diocese.

"Leave it to me," said Dominic, "I know what I'm doing. We have to sow the seed, not hoard it."

He had told his friars to trust completely in God. Now he was giving them their first practical lesson. It was swiftly justified, for young men came flocking to join the preachers, many of them students from the new universities where Dominic sent his men to learn and, very soon, to teach.

Dominic himself, meanwhile, tried to give up his position as Master-General of the new Order. He felt that his work was done and that there were others competent to take his place. Once again, he asked permission to go as a humble missionary to Russia.

The Pope, I need hardly say, would not hear of it. He kept Dominic in Rome to reorganize the religious life of the nuns there, which had become undisciplined to the point of chaos. During this visit, Dominic is said to have raised to life a young man killed by a fall from his horse.

The nuns safely reorganized, Dominic returned to his Dominicans, as people soon began to call them. This produced a neat Latin pun; for *Dominicanes* read *Domini Canes*—"Dogs of the Lord". And so they were; hounds in their unflagging pursuit of truth, watchdogs in their zeal to defend it. The motto of the Order is, to this day, just the one word, *Veritas*.

Though he continued to practise his own severe penances, Dominic was much more gentle with the youngsters who came to join him. Even when he was ill, he himself slept blanketless on the ground, just as he had always done. With the Brother who nursed him he had a regular battle of wits over this, which the Brother always lost. Yet at night he would move through the dormitories replacing the bedclothes of novices who had kicked them off in their sleep. He fasted, but he made the friars eat properly.

He was not, as many people suppose, a somber or severe man. During the evidence for his canonization, those who knew him refer again and again to his happy and affectionate nature. He invariably had a fund of stories to tell, and anyone he met immediately felt at home. "He was always good to talk to in time of trouble," a witness testified. Another said that if Dominic ever looked sad, it was always at another's misfortune.

Even when he had to impose a penance on anyone, there were never any sulks, so kindly was it done. When he was told that some young friars were suffering from scruples over their observance of the Rule, Dominic declared that he would personally rip up every copy of the Rule with a knife rather than let it cause suffering to anyone. It did not, he insisted, bind under pain of sin.

There were more miracles. One friar told how, when he and Dominic were caught in a heavy rainstorm, both had been kept dry though the rain continued to pour three paces ahead. On another occasion, it was said, a party of English pilgrims, suddenly thrown from a boat, were rescued after being miraculously brought to the surface. As his fame grew, people cut bits off his habit when they gathered to hear him preach.

This last period of Dominic's life lasted for only five years; during that time he lived mostly at Bologna. He was his Order spread through France, Spain and Italy; he saw friars depart for Greece, Denmark, Hungary and England.

At the beginning of August, 1221, Dominic realized that he was dying. Calling the Brothers round him, he begged them always to preserve charity, humility and poverty; never, never were they to accept property of any kind.

He thanked God that he had always kept his vow of chastity. "But," he added, "I must confess that I have enjoyed talking to young women more than to old ones."

This very human admission troubled the canonization commission a good deal. In the end, they kept it out of the official record in case it should damage his reputation!

Dominic died at Bologna on August 6th, the Feast of the Transfiguration, in a borrowed habit and a borrowed bed, poor to the last. His feast-day is August 4.

In the years that followed, the Order of preachers grew more rapidly than ever, though not everyone was pleased by this. "They have the world for their cell and the ocean for their cloister," wrote Matthew Paris, a grouchy English Benedictine. He meant it as a jibe, but Dominic would have been delighted. No one could have summed up his ideal more succinctly.

In 1943, as the Allied armies advanced on Bologna, Dominic's remains were moved to a place of safety and Pope Pius XII took the opportunity to have them scientifically examined. The findings, together with early portraits, give us a very accurate idea of Dominic's physical appearance.

He was not very tall—five feet three-and-a-quarter inches—but his face, with his hooked Castilian nose and his high cheekbones, must have been very striking. Yet it was not his physical appearance that drew so many to forsake heresy, or to join him in the work which he had begun. The secret lay within.

"He embraced all men with his great love," said his first biographer, "and because he loved the world the world loved him."

The Angelic Doctor

Dominic had been about 30 years dead when a group of friars wearing the habit of his Order paused to rest by a roadside spring in Tuscany. As they sipped the water gratefully, a small dust-cloud appeared in the distance. Before they knew what was happening, a group of mounted knights had thundered up and seized the youngest friar, a tubby lad of 19.

"Come on, Thomas," said their leader firmly. "We are going home."

Thomas clearly did not want to go home. Despite his girth he put up a fierce struggle, especially when the knights tried to rip the habit from his back. The other friars watched, helpless; the end of the bizarre rough-house was never in doubt. But when they finally bore him away, Thomas d'Aquino was still wearing his habit.

He spent the next two years imprisoned in the family fortress of Monte San Giovanni, near Naples. During that time his brothers—for it was they who had brought him back—did everything to persuade him to give up the poverty-stricken friars and become a Benedictine monk instead. It was, they insisted, his duty. Why, with his talents and his background, he must surely become Abbot of Monte Cassino. Then he could restore the family's bedraggled fortunes.

Thomas met all their arguments with a smile and a shake of the head, and went right on studying. Wherever he was, whatever was happening, Thomas always went on studying. It had been that way since he first learned to read.

Seeing that argument was getting them nowhere, the brothers tried a more drastic method. They sent a prostitute into his cell to seduce him from his vow of chastity. That was the only time that Thomas became angry. He drove the poor woman from the room with a blazing torch.

Thomas, whom we know best as Thomas Aquinas, was born in the other family home, a few miles away at Roccasecca, around the year 1225. His father's people were Lombard nobles, his mother's Norman. Sent to school at Monte Cassino, he was still only five when he first asked the monks: "What is God?" Again and again he asked the same question. In a sense, he was to go on asking it to the end of his life.

It was at the University of Naples that Thomas first met the new Order of preachers. A university in the Middle Ages was just as cosmopolitan as a modern one, and the boy from Roccasecca listened raptly to the lectures of such teachers as Peter the Irishman and Martin of Denmark.

But it was to the Dominican house of studies that he returned again and again, to talk theology with the friars, to argue and to learn. Soon he knew for certain. This was where he belonged; here, with the new Order of preachers.

Though they probably did not let him see it, the Dominicans must have been quite as impressed with their postulant as he was with them, for here indeed was a mind out of the ordinary. He went skilfully to the root of every question, testing and probing with a maturity far beyond his years. Though one of the youngest students on campus, already he was coaching the less gifted with their work.

In 1244 the German Master-General, John the Teuton, visited Naples. From him, probably, Thomas received the habit that he later fought so hard to keep by that dusty roadside in Tuscany.

At the end of two years, it was plain to his family that Thomas would not give in and so, reluctantly, he was sent back to the Dominicans. According to one story, his mother so arranged matters that he could lower himself from a window by a sheet. Face would be saved if Thomas were seen to have escaped!

Though he never did become a Benedictine, he sent their order a consolation prize—his sister Marotta, who became an abbess. A worldly little creature, she had been recruited to talk Thomas out of the Dominicans. Instead, he talked her into a convent.

The year 1248 found the young friar studying at Cologne under St. Albert the Great, the German Dominican who still ranks among the Order's greatest thinkers— second only to Thomas himself.

Unlike Thomas, who was strictly a philosopher and a theologian, Albert was also a scientist. Physics, alchemy, natural history, astronomy—all these he taught and studied along with philosophy, theology and the Bible. In particular he was a keen student of Aristotle, another thinker with an omnivorous mind, who had only recently been translated into Latin.

Thomas, too, became convinced that Aristotle was the most important of all the Greek philosophers. In fact, when he wrote about him later, he always called him simply "the Philosopher", just as he called St. Paul "the Apostle".

Meanwhile, he was suffering, with great good humor, the jibes of fellow-students who had christened him "the dumb ox". Because he was stout and moved slowly, and because his mind always seemed elsewhere, they assumed that he was slow-witted.

One day, a student kinder than the rest offered to explain a point in one of Albert's lectures to the poor dumb ox. He had somehow got the impression that Thomas was puzzled by it. Having begun his lucid exposition, he quickly got himself tied in knots. In the end, Thomas had to extricate him, leaving the well-meaning student amazed at his grasp of the subject. So the ox was not so dumb after all!

Indeed he was not—as Albert himself found when he heard Thomas defend a thesis before his fellow-students. "Dumb ox!" exclaimed Albert. "I'm telling you, this ox's bellowing is going to be heard throughout the world!"

Unlike almost all the other saints in this book, Thomas had a quiet life, the life of a scholar and a preacher. Once he had won the battle with his family, all his remaining battles were intellectual ones.

Yet even these had a certain drama. In "baptizing" Aristotle, in making his philosophy serve the Christian message, Thomas was taking a bold and courageous step. As one recent writer has said, it was rather as though a Catholic philosopher of the present day were to press Karl Marx into service!

Not only was Aristotle a pagan who lived before Christ; he was a pagan who boldly used his reason on questions which Christians had always considered strictly within the province of divine revelation. He used his reason, for example, on the fundamental question, is there a God? He came to the conclusion that indeed there was; although Aristotle's God was not, of course, the Christian God whom we know, but an abstract entity who must exist somewhere but who had told us nothing about himself.

To earlier Christian thinkers—to Bernard of Clairvaux,

for example—this kind of approach was highly undesirable and, indeed, dangerous. To them it seemed wrong to import reason into theology when we had been given revelation to tell us what we needed to know. Probably, deep down, they feared a clash between the two.

But there was no clash, Thomas insisted. Nor could there be, since reason and revelation came equally from God. Truth is truth, by whatever means we receive it.

"The existence of God can be proved in five ways." With this confident assertion Thomas launches into his most famous exposition in the first part of the *Summa Theologica,* the textbook which he wrote for Catholic undergraduates. His "five ways" are an excellent example of his use of Aristotle's technique.

Very simply stated, they go like this:

1. Things in the world are subject to change. (Thomas said *some* things; we know that everything is!) Yet nothing can change without some outside agency: the sun must melt the ice; the bat must strike the ball. And these outside agents, the sun and the bat, are themselves subject to change; they also are moved by forces outside themselves. Somewhere, therefore, there must be a Changer who is not himself changed, a Mover who is not himself moved. And this someone we call God.

2. This argument is very similar to the first. We are surrounded by cause and effect, each cause being an effect of some prior cause. Somewhere there must be a First Cause.

3. Everything we can think of depends for its existence upon something else. We cannot point to anything and say: "That is absolutely necessary, it is the reason for its own existence." But everything cannot be like this, otherwise nothing would ever

come into existence in the first place. So there must be one Necessary Being in which the existence of all the unnecessary beings is grounded.

4. We frequently speak of perfection, but never actually experience it. We have never known perfect goodness or perfect beauty. But the Perfect must exist, or how could we have the ideal?

5. Throughout the universe we are surrounded by evidence of purpose or design, from the structure of an insect's wing to the motions of the heavenly bodies. If there is a design, there must be a Designer.

These arguments do not, indeed, lead us to the Blessed Trinity, but they do demonstrate that faith in God, far from being contrary to reason, is in harmony with it. They are also a useful weapon against atheism and agnosticism, which are shown to be fundamentally irrational.

Thomas did most of his teaching at the University of Paris, though he was for a time called to Rome as theological adviser to the papal court. Apart from the *Summa Theologica,* his other major work was the *Summa Contra Gentiles,* a defence of the Christian faith directed to Islam.

In all his thinking he sought a grand design: he tried to discover the relationship between God, man and the universe, using his reason both on what we can experience for ourselves and on what God has taught us about Himself.

Everything, therefore, is within his range: God, man, angels, devils, the world, virtue, sin, human society—all are analysed and fitted together in the general scheme. His method is to pose a question and then give his reasoned reply. He proceeds carefully and logically from question to question, and never ducks an issue. "Does the State have the right to put heretics to death?" he asks on one page. On another: "Do the blessed in Heaven rejoice in the sufferings of the damned?"

Most of the stories about Thomas's later life concern his prodigious absent-mindedness. Beside him, Archimedes in his bath-towel was the soul of self-possession.

On a famous occasion, he was invited to dine with St. Louis, the King of France, but during the meal he said not one word. Towards the end, without warning, he brought his fist down with a crash on to the table. "That's the answer to the Manichaeans!" he declared triumphantly. The King, fascinated, ordered pen and paper to be placed before him.

Again, when a cardinal called to see him, Thomas walked into the room and took not the slightest notice of the great man. When a colleague pulled his sleeve, he smiled and apologized. "I never realized that I had left my cell," he explained.

Like Bernard of Clairvaux, he achieved a truly yogic concentration. Once, when a wound in his leg was cauterized, he did not feel the iron at all, so deeply was he meditating during the operation.

Because of his size, and because of his meek and gentle disposition, lesser men sometimes made fun or took advantage of him. Perhaps the most famous story is that of the friar who shouted: "Look, Thomas, there's a cow flying over the rooftop!"

Thomas, sunk in thought as usual, looked up involuntarily. When the man jeered at his credulity, Thomas's reply was mild but crushing.

"I was more ready to believe that a cow could fly," he said, "than that a friar could tell a deliberate lie."

When a newcomer to the house asked leave to go into

the city, the prior replied that he should take as companion the first friar he met on his way out. It happened to be Thomas, then at the height of his fame.

The great theologian accompanied him without demur, and apologized humbly when berated for walking so slowly. Only when they returned to base did the newcomer discover who it was that he had treated so churlishly.

Thomas was, of course, much more than a great theologian: he was a saint and a mystic. This was the great paradox of his life: that while he was teaching the Church how to use reason in the service of faith, while he was building his great rational system of theology, God was revealing Himself to Thomas by means which were above and beyond reason. It was frequently observed that while he was celebrating Mass, he would weep and become lost in prayer at the consecration.

When the new feast of Corpus Christi was introduced, it was Thomas who was asked to compose the Office. The most famous of all his writings are not his great theological works, but the hymns *O Salutaris* and *Tantum Ergo*, which are sung every week by Catholics who have never heard of the *Summa Theologica*. Two other beautiful hymns, *Adoro Te Devote* and *Pange Lingua* are also his.

At least twice, it was said, Christ spoke to him from the crucifix, each time to compliment him on his work.

"You have written well of me, Thomas," said the Figure the second time. "What will you have as a reward?"

"Nothing but yourself, Lord," Thomas replied.

Towards the end of his life he had a mystical experience so profound that he could write no more. "All my work now seems like so much straw," he told his friend, Brother Reginald. The *Summa Theologica* was never finished.

In 1274, when Thomas was preaching in dear familiar

Naples, Pope Gregory X asked him to attend the Council of Lyons, which had been called in an attempt to heal the schism between Catholics and Orthodox. Thomas, though far from well, obediently set out for France.

Traveling along the Appian Way towards Rome, he became so ill that Brother Reginald had him carried into the Cistercian monastery of Fossa Nuova. When he saw the monks making up the fire in his room, he was disturbed. "It can't be right that holy men should bring firewood for me," he said.

A little later he was asked if there was anything he would like, and he surprised everyone by asking for herrings. Throughout his life he had shown no interest in food; indeed, for most of the time he had no idea what he was eating. But now he craved herrings.

Happily, herrings were soon found and not long after he had eaten them, Thomas died very peacefully, worn out by overwork. He was not yet 50.

Thomas is often called the Angelic Doctor and the name is apt. Rarely, if ever, have such gentle innocence and such profound learning been combined in one man. He is the patron of all Catholic schools and for centuries his books were the basis of priests' training throughout the Church. Unhappily, young men are now being ordained who know little of his work—a sad state of affairs but, I trust, a temporary one. The Church must, it is true, always be open to new insights. But Thomas is, and always will be, her perennial philosopher.

The Blessed Girl of the People

On a sunny afternoon in 1354, two young children were hurrying hand-in-hand through the narrow alleys of Siena towards their home in the Street of the Wool-Dyers. Their day had been spent with a married sister, but they had to be back for tea.

By St. Dominic's Church the younger, seven-year old Catherine suddenly slipped her hand free and stopped, gazing upwards at the sky.

Her brother, Stefano, stopped and turned. For a second he was taken aback. There was a strange expression on Catherine's face—an expression he had never seen before. "What's wrong?" he asked, slightly alarmed. "What are you staring at?"

Catherine did not reply. Indeed, she did not seem to have heard the question.

Stefano grasped her hand again firmly, impatience replacing alarm.

"Come on," he snapped, tugging her forward. You know Mom will holler if we're late!"

To his surprise, Catherine burst into tears.

"Oh, Stefano," she sobbed. "If you had seen what I have just seen, you wouldn't have pulled me away like that!"

What Catherine had seen, she insisted later, was a vision of Jesus, accompanied by three of the saints—Peter, Paul and John. He had raised his hand over her in a blessing.

Seven-year-olds who see visions in the sky are not generally taken seriously, nor were they in medieval Italy. Catherine Benincasa got a predictable scolding and there, everyone assumed, the matter would end.

But there it did not end.

From the moment of her strange experience, Catherine became a different child. Previously she had been happy and fun-loving, but not especially pious. Now she still played happily in Siena's quaint, sunlit streets. But before long, she would invariably lead her friends off to a dark corner of the big house where her father kept both his family and his vats. There they would pray and, at Catherine's instigation, they would scourge each other.

Even worse, in the eyes of Catherine's mother, her healthy girl was steadfastly refusing to eat. She had developed a mania about fasting and was living almost entirely on bread, fruit and vegetables.

As Catherine grew into her teens, Donna Lapa got seriously worried, as well she might. Poor woman, she had enough to care about as it was. Her husband, Giacomo, was a good man and he made good money, but Lapa had borne his 25 children and she was no longer young.

Of the 13 surviving youngsters, the older end were already happily married, and Lapa wanted the same for Catherine. It really did not seem too much to ask. If the child would only look after herself, she might easily make a good match. She could be beautiful, with her fair skin and her mass of golden hair, so unusual in Tuscany. Instead of this, thanks to her weird way of life, she was growing up looking pinched and sickly.

When marriage was mentioned, Catherine replied that she intended to remain a virgin. That was what Jesus wanted of her; that was the meaning of the vision in the sky.

"Are you telling me," her mother demanded, "that you took a vow of chastity at seven?"

"Yes," said Catherine, "that's right."

Donna Lapa screamed.

Hard-headed Giacomo did not, as another father might have done, try to beat the nonsense out of his mad daughter. Instead, he supported her—insisted that Catherine should, in that over-crowded house, have a room of her own so that she could pray and do penance in privacy. He promised, too, that she should not be forced into marriage. When his wife upbraided him, he muttered something about seeing a dove hover over the girl's head.

Giacomo was right to take his daughter seriously. God had work for her. Incredibly, he had chosen this not-very-bright young girl to be the adviser of two Popes and many humbler folk. He had chosen the wool-dyer's daughter to lead the supreme Pontiff, after 70 years of exile, back to his rightful place in Rome. And the vision was the beginning of her destiny.

For the sake of peace, Catherine agreed to go on holiday with her mother to the resort of Vignone, where the mineral springs might do her good and, hopefully, give her a healthier outlook on life. Once there, Catherine wandered into the waters and, ignoring the shouts of the attendants, walked straight into the area where the springs came boiling from the ground.

Did she do it purposely, to disfigure herself and so remove the threat of marriage once and for all? We do not know. At any rate, she was not disfigured, either by the scalding or by the attack of smallpox which she suffered immediately afterwards.

Happily, her illness did bring about a truce in the Benincasa homestead. Mother abandoned her objections
and Catherine was received into the Third Order of St.
Dominic.

She did not, as you might expect, enter a convent; she
went right on living at home, as most tertiaries do today.
But her life was as enclosed as that of any Carmelite
nun—in fact, more so. For three years she never went
outside her "cell" except to go to Mass and confession.
She lived on a spoonful of herbs and slept for only two
hours each night. She spoke to no one but her confessor.

At the end of the three years came another vision. Our
Lord appeared to her, with the Blessed Virgin, and put a
beautiful ring on her finger as He took her for his bride.
He told her to be bold and decisive in everything she did
for him. Whatever happened, she would win.

He also told her to rejoin her family and she did. She
ate with them, she helped her mother with the house-
work, she played with her growing band of little nieces
and nephews. "If I weren't ashamed to do so," she declared happily, "I'd spend all my time playing with
them!"

From one extreme she went to the other. Whereas she
had previously refused to see anybody, now she saw
everybody. Priests, poets, painters, students—all came
flocking to her little cell to talk, to pray and, often, to
sing. One smile from Catherine, and you were her friend
forever; you had to keep on going back to see her, to
listen to the things she said. Just one look, and she could
change your entire way of life. Nobody had to tell her
their problems, their fears, their temptations, their sins.
She knew just by looking.

And what of the neighbors, the people who had
watched her grow up? Were they proud and amazed to
discover that they had a saint and a mystic in their midst?

Quite the reverse. Soon there were nudges and whispers. What was she doing, this girl who went around dressed like a nun, but who entertained people— including young men—until all hours of the night? And what hold had she got over them anyway? A few actually murmured the dreaded word. Catherine, surely, must be a witch!

Not that she spent all her time holding court. She also worked as a volunteer nurse at Siena's Hospital of Santa Maria della Scala and there, everyone agreed, she was an able and a cheerful helper—an extra ray of sunshine in the crowded wards.

Yet it was one of those she had nursed—a spiteful old woman called Tecca—who now led the whispering campaign against her. Soon they had something to whisper about. Catherine, through no fault of her own, became the center of a major scandal.

A young friar, Pietro di Mastro Lando, had developed a hopeless passion for her, which Catherine dealt with as sympathetically as she could. But in the end, poor Pietro killed himself. The tragedy brought things to a head.

Catherine was summoned before the senior Sisters of the Third Order to answer the allegations against her. She refused to defend herself in any detail. She only repeated, again and again, that she was still a virgin.

The row reached the ears of the Pope, Gregory XI, in his palace at Avignon. He instructed the Dominican Master-General, Elia of Toulouse, to conduct a full investigation. Catherine was summoned to Florence, where the Order was about to hold a General Chapter.

The proceedings were held along forensic lines, with a friar speaking for the prosecution and another for the defense. The "jury" consisted of the 500 chapter delegates, assembled from all parts of Europe. If the verdict went against her, Catherine would be expelled from the Order.

Just as before, she refused to speak on her own behalf; she left everything to the friar appointed to defend her. But it was her own serene dignity which made the deepest impression. All charges were dismissed.

Indeed, the whole ordeal brought Catherine a big gain, for the Dominicans gave her a special spiritual director: Blessed Raymond of Capua, a wise and learned friar who became her lifelong friend and the first of her many biographers.

Returning to Siena, Catherine and her companions found the city in the grip of the plague. Day and night she nursed the sick, encouraging them, praying for them and, when they died, burying them with her own hands. Many of her own relatives were among the victims; she buried no fewer than eight of those little nieces and nephews she had loved so much. "These children I shall never lose," she said simply, and went on working.

Several times she effected cures. "Come on, Matteo, get up," she told one gravely ill friend. "This is no time to be lying in a soft bed!" When Raymond was struck down, she cured him too.

Anyone condemned to death would be sure to have a visit from *La Beata Popolana*—"The Blessed Girl of the People" as many were beginning to call her.

Among these unfortunates was a young knight from Perugia, Nicholas di Toldo, sentenced to death for sedition. At first he was bitter and rejected all spiritual help; Catherine won him over completely. He died laughing and confident as she prayed for him on the scaffold.

People came from far and near with their problems, including problems of conscience. On the Pope's instruction, the Dominicans kept a team of priests standing by to hear the confessions which followed. Though Catherine was illiterate until her late teens, and even then had trouble learning to read, her theological knowledge was profound. When her enemies sent skilled doctors of divinity to trap her with difficult questions, she sent them home with their egos badly bruised.

By now her fame had spread far beyond her home town. In February, 1375, she visited Pisa and lectured the city fathers on their shortcomings as Christian rulers!

During this visit, she received Holy Communion from Raymond in the Church of St. Christina. As she gazed at the crucifix afterwards, five blood-red rays came from it towards her, piercing her hands, feet and side. These stigmata remained invisible to everyone but herself and she kept them secret, confiding only in Raymond. When she died, however, the wounds became clearly visible.

In Pisa, just as at home in Siena, Catherine launched a spiritual revival, bringing people back to the Sacraments, helping with their problems, settling their disputes. But now, a much bigger dispute was blowing up on the international scene.

Though he lived in France, the Pope still ruled a large part of Italy. For some time there had been discontent with the legates who carried on government for him. Finally it erupted. Florence, Bologna and a number of other cities rose against their absentee sovereign.

The Pope appealed to the Florentines, and when that did not do any good he hired a rough English mercenary, Sir John Hawkwood, and his army of cutthroats. As they camped menacingly outside Florence, Gregory laid the whole city under an interdict, which effectively barred nearly everyone from Mass and the Sacraments. Gravely alarmed, the Florentines called Catherine in as mediator.

It was not only by repute that Gregory XI knew the little mystic from Siena. Catherine had already written to him—not one letter but several, in which she had urged him again and again to move from Avignon to Rome. The

Church's troubles, she was convinced, would not end until he did.

These letters, which we still have, are probably the most remarkable any Pope ever received. Catherine talks to the Pontiff as though he were a foolish parent about to mess up the family fortunes and she, the favorite daughter, were chiding him for his own good. Though she addresses him constantly as *Babbo*—Dad—her tone is distinctly maternal:

> Dear *Babbo,* sweet Christ on earth, why don't you follow the example of your namesake Gregory the Great? Just look what he achieved, yet he was a man like yourself! And God is the same now as He was then. All you need is grit, determination, and a real hunger for the salvation of souls!

If Catherine could treat the Pope like that, small wonder that her friends back in Siena—even those who were older than herself—always called her *Mamma!*

In fact, Gregory needed a friend like Catherine to put some backbone into him. He was not a fool, but neither was he a tough character. Yet few Popes have had bigger problems to face. A Frenchman himself, he had been created a cardinal at 19 through family influence, and elected Pope before he was even a priest. He had, nevertheless, already decided to move the papacy back to Rome—had even vowed it secretly. But he was surrounded by powerful men who were determined that he should stay put, and he had not yet found the courage to resist them.

When Catherine arrived in Avignon, she got a scornful welcome from the proud ladies of the papal court. For once, her magnetism did not work. Who was this tradesman's daughter, who thought she could tell the Pope how to run the Church? Catherine looked calmly at them and wrinkled her nose. The perfume of sin, she said, stank in her nostrils.

When at last she met Gregory face to face, she was no less blunt than in her letters. "Do what you have promised to do!" she told him. Gregory was considerably shaken, for he had told nobody of his vow.

On September 13, 1376, Gregory at last set out for the Eternal City. The long exile was over.

Unhappily, he lived for only another 18 months. His successor, Urban VI, was a hard Neapolitan cardinal who did not need a Catherine to tell him that even though the Pope was back in Rome, there was still much wrong with the Church, and with the clergy especially. Just the same, Urban, too, got some motherly advice:

> When you are appointing bishops, appoint men who seek God and not a fat income . . . Please don't mind my writing to you about such matters. I do it purely for the honor of God and for your own salvation.

Did Urban, who in fact set about some energetic reforms, resent being lectured in this fashion? Not at all. He called Catherine to Rome to be his adviser.

Meanwhile, Catherine had directed another of her lectures at the King of France. Instead of warring against England, she told him, he should be away fighting the Turk in the Holy Land:

> You ought to be ashamed, and so should the other Christian rulers! No wonder many of your subjects hold you in contempt. Here you are, fighting one

another while the enemy is left alone. It is an insult to God!

Hawksmoor, the English freebooter, got a similar letter. Instead of cursing and swearing at the sender, he sent a courteous reply.

Throughout her short life, Catherine remained convinced that a new crusade was the best way to heal Europe's divisions and to bring about the conversion of Islam, and she badgered rulers and Popes alike to sound the call to arms.

But now the Church was threatened by a new crisis. French cardinals, furious at Urban's election and dismayed by his reforms, elected a rival "pope" of their own and installed him at Avignon. It was not the first time that two claimants had contended for the papacy, but this time the schism was to last for 70 years.

For Catherine it was the beginning of her final agony. Living only on the Sacred Host, which she received each morning, sleeping for only an hour each night, she worked without ceasing to try to restore peace to the Church. But all her letters, all her pleading with great men, were of no avail.

To God she offered her life as a sacrifice, and it was accepted. On a January evening in 1380, while dictating a letter to Pope Urban, she had a stroke. Recovering consciousness, she suffered terrible visions—or hallucinations—in which she seemed to be wrestling with demons. She saw the Church, in the form of a great ship, crushing her under its weight.

She had a second strike while praying in St. Peter's and three weeks later, on April 29, 1380, she died, aged 33.

"Everyone loves Catherine of Siena because she was always and everywhere a woman in every fiber of her being," wrote an American Dominican, Father Thomas M. Schwertner. That is indeed true. Yet she turned aside from convent and kitchen to play a man's part in history. Today's campaigners for women's rights could do worse than make Catherine their patron saint.

Portrait of a Lady

This story begins just like the last one, with a little girl and her brother hurrying along hand in hand. These two are not, however, going home for tea—quite the opposite. They are running away.

Their destination is Africa, for Africa is where the Moors live. Once there, they will get themselves beheaded, win a martyr's crown and so reach Heaven by the shortest possible route.

Teresa and Rodrigo did not get very far; indeed, they were scarcely out of Avila before they were caught and brought back to their comfortable home, a palace near the ramparts in the Jewish quarter. Only now there are no Jews. Fear of the Inquisition had put them all to flight.

The years pass. Rodrigo has gone with his six brothers to help to run Spain's empire in the New World. Teresa, now twenty-one, is a raven-haired Castillian beauty; gay, generous, fond of jewels, clothes, dances and parties. As she gets into a carriage one evening, a young man admires her feet.

"Take a good look at them," says Teresa, eyes flashing merrily, "You won't get another chance!"

He won't, either. For Senorita Teresa de Cepeda Davilla y Ahumada, is about to become a Carmelite nun.

Well, naturally, you may be thinking. A child who wanted to be a martyr was clearly headed for a life in religion. In fact Teresa never thought of becoming a nun until she was well into her teens, and when she began to suspect that it was what God wanted she was not at all pleased; indeed she was very cross with Him, as she herself tells us in her autobiography.

Nevertheless a nun she became, in Avila's Convent of the Incarnation.

Several times in this book we have found religious life in something of a mess, and so it was in sixteenth-century Spain. Few nuns, if any, were really immoral. Some were holy. But old ideals had faded; sisters wore jewellery, went out for meals, constantly entertained visitors—even had boy-friends.

All this troubled Teresa little if at all; it scarcely struck her that there was anything wrong about it. Nobody now gave much thought to the original Carmelite Rule, and it was only by chance that she learned that nuns were not supposed to have any property of their own.

Within two years of her entering the convent, Teresa's health collapsed. She wasted away until she was little more than a bag of bones; so weak was she that she could scarcely walk around. She received the Last Sacraments, but did not die. For the next three years she lived the life of an invalid. What the nature of her illness might have been we can only guess.

Her mother, Doña Beatriz, had died when Teresa was fourteen. Soon after the young nun recovered, her father, Don Alfonso, also passed on. She had loved them both dearly and later, during one of her many visions, she saw both of them in Heaven. But visions were in the future.

While convalescing in her uncle's country home, Teresa began to read religious classics and, for the first time in her life, developed the habit of mental prayer. It did not last. Once recovered and back in the convent, she lapsed into a tepid state, going through the formal devotions but making no real effort to pray seriously.

She continued like this for fifteen unhappy years—unhappy because she felt keenly the ambiguity of her position. "On the one side I could hear God calling me," she wrote later, "on the other, I was pulled along by the spirit of the world. It was so distressing that I don't know how I endured it."

The turning-point came on a day in the year 1555. Sister Teresa, now a woman of forty, went into the convent chapel and found herself gazing at a picture of Christ in agony that had been obtained for a special feast-day. Throwing herself down before it, she vowed that she would not get up again until Jesus resolved the conflict inside her and made her his own.

Her prayer was answered much more dramatically than ever she bargained for. Teresa's new life had begun.

"God deliver me from sullen saints," she said once, and the words could be taken as her lifelong motto. Her new life was a twofold journey: an inward journey towards God and an outward journey round Spain. Yet whatever trials she suffered—and they were many and great—her sense of humor never deserted her. Even when she complained, she did it with a smile. "If this is how you treat your friends, Lord," she said once, in a fit of exasperation "it's little wonder that you have so few!"

It was in 1562, after years of preparation, that Teresa began the task of reforming the Carmelites.

In one of the visions which were now part of her life, Our Lord had told her to set up a new convent based on the order's original Rule, and dedicate it to St. Joseph. With money obtained from her brother, Teresa secretly bought an old building in another part of Avila and prepared to move in.

As soon as her intention became known, the storm broke! Who did she think she was, demanded her sisters at Incarnation, setting up a rival institution of her own? Were they not good enough for her? If she could find money for a new convent, why could she not have found it for them instead?

Then the town council learned that Teresa's convent, instead of being endowed, was to exist on whatever people chose to send it. The council, wanting no holy beggars in Avila, went to law in an effort to scotch the whole project. Teresa was tempted to accept an endowment just until St. Joseph's was established and feeling died down. Our Lord, appearing again, warned her to do nothing of the kind. "Once you accept it, they'll never let you get rid of it," He declared.

This businesslike conversation was quite typical: many of Teresa's visions were of the most matter-of-fact kind. When it looked as though work on the convent might not be finished after all, through lack of money, St. Joseph appeared and told her to hire the workmen: money would be forthcoming. And it was.

With all difficulties overcome, Teresa and four other sisters at last moved in. Teresa did not want to be prioress, but the others insisted. Five years later, the Carmelite general arrived from Rome and told Teresa to found more houses—not only for women, but for men too. Now the Carmelite Reform was really under way, but there was still plenty of trouble ahead.

In her work for the friars, Teresa found an invaluable helper, a young priest named Juan de Yepes. The world knows him as St. John of the Cross, one of the greatest of all mystical poets.

For Teresa herself, life was now spent largely in springless carts, bumping along the roads of Spain setting up and nurturing the new convents. Altogether, she saw 29 houses established, seventeen for women and twelve for men. "And all," as she herself said, "without even a penny to buy one."

Like so many of the great mystics, Teresa was an intensely practical person. In this she differed from John of the Cross and his two companions, who set up the first reformed friary at Duruelo with five hour-glasses as their only furniture! When she arrived and saw them, Teresa laughed and laughed.

Other experiences were not so funny—at least not at the time. One night she and her party got mixed up among some bulls which were being driven into town for next day's bullfight. Their donkey disappeared, carrying all the money given them as alms, and Teresa herself got separated from the rest, who wandered about all night looking for her.

As part of their regime of absolute poverty, Teresa's followers abandoned shoes and wore instead the rope sandals of the poor Spanish peasants. They became known as "discalced" (unshod) Carmelites—a name that they have retained to the present day.

Inevitably there were tensions between the discalced and the calced—although the latter did reform themselves later on. Meanwhile, Teresa was about to get a shock. Suddenly her superiors asked her to return to Avila to become prioress of her old convent, Incarnation.

It was an astonishing decision, since Teresa had parted the worst of friends with the sisters there. Yet it was also a necessary one, for the convent had gone from bad to worse. When the new prioress presented herself, the scenes were ugly indeed. Howls of rage greeted her. Nuns wept, fainted, became hysterical, insisted that their rights had been trampled on, demanded to know why they had not been consulted.

Teresa begged to be relieved of her position, but the provincial insisted she go back. So she did—and this time she put a statue of Our Lady in the prioress's chair, put the keys of the convent in its hands, and took the next place herself. Calmly, she told them that the post was not of her own seeking, but that since she had to fulfil it, she would serve them all to the last drop of her blood.

Few could resist Teresa's charm for long. Soon they were all eating out of her hand. They continued to do so for the three years of her reign.

Teresa of Avila was yet another dynamic saint whose real desire was to remain in the cloister and devote herself to prayer—which, after all, was what she intended when she became a nun in the first place. She loved community life and was always in demand at recreation-time; the other sisters would beg her to join them and often she did, even when she was tired or overwhelmed with paper-work. Not only did she joke and tell stories; sometimes she danced and played the tambourine.

In later life, when her beauty had faded, she allowed a friar to paint her portrait. "May God forgive you, Fray Juan," she said when he had finished, "What you made me suffer in sitting for you—and now you have made me look so very ugly!"

Like Catherine of Siena, she doted on children—especially Teresita, an eight-year-old niece sent from South America to be cared for by Teresa and her nuns. "She certainly knows how to amuse us—she describes the Indians and the voyage far better than I could," wrote her distinguished aunt.

It is with a chill that we read words like these—and then remember that Teresa's Spain, so full of grandeur and gaiety, was also a place where heretics were burned at the stake. In the convent of Seville one day, a poor, disturbed novice denounced Teresa and the other sisters to the local Inquisitor.

Teresa's friends were terrified. What if he learned of

her visions? People who had visions were always suspect—and now she had been reported for heresy! Fear grew when officials arrived from the Inquisitor's Office to search the convent.

Teresa, who was afraid of nobody and certainly not of any inquisitor, went off to find the gentleman for herself. Yes indeed she had had visions, she told him; in fact they were something of an embarrassment to her, since they were apt to come at the most awkward times. She believed that they were from God but she was perfectly prepared to subject herself to the Inquisition's judgment in the matter, since she did not wish to be deluded by Satan.

The Inquisitor listened courteously and suggested that Teresa write her life-story, so that a priest of eminent holiness could read it and decide whether her visions were genuine or not.

So Teresa sat down and produced her autobiography, one of the great spiritual books of all time, in which she described, not only her visions, but the process by which God taught her mental prayer and drew her ever closer towards himself.

The visions, certainly, are remarkable; as I have already indicated, Teresa conversed frequently with Christ on terms of the utmost familiarity and she also saw the Blessed Virgin and many of the saints. There were visits both to Heaven and to Hell, where she was shown the place which the devils had reserved for her, should she ever fall into their hands.

Writing about this, Teresa admits that it was a very frightening experience, but adds that she does not think about it often. When she saw Satan, she called him "Goose".

Visions, she insists, are of secondary importance since they belong to the senses. What matters is prayer, and above all mental prayer, by which everyone can grow in the love of God. That was the main purpose of her Reform—to get nuns and friars to pray properly. Correcting abuses and enforcing the Rule were only means to that end.

Eventually she asked God to send her no more visions but to lead her soul forward by more mature means. Her request was granted. In time, she found herself with an inner awareness of the Blessed Trinity far more real to her than any knowledge that came via her senses.

In her autobiography, and in the other books which she wrote, Teresa analyses the nature and technique of mental prayer with an assurance which places her among the foremost spiritual teachers. Thomas Aquinas would certainly have admired her clarity and insight, as did many of her contemporaries.

Many, but not all. Her very brilliance brought her enemies. "Do not mention that woman to me!" fumed an irate papal nuncio. "She is a disobedient and wilful female who spreads her pernicious ideas under the pretence of devotion, leaves the cloister against orders and teaches theology as though she were a Doctor of the Church!"

In this he defamed Teresa, who never at any time left the cloister without permission. She had the approval of the Pope and her superiors in all that she did.

Nevertheless, to the end of her life there were those within her own order who continued to resent her bitterly. In her last month on earth, one prioress showed her the door of the convent, and another was so unfriendly that, ill and fasting as she was, she left next morning.

The next stop, at Alba, was the last. When the sisters there asked if she wished to die at Avila, her reply was characteristic: "Surely they will give me a little earth here!"

She was sixty-four when she died, worn out but still on her travels, saying farewell with a joke. The date: October 4th, 1582.

She was canonised only forty years later, with a speed that must have made her smile. And somewhere, surely, her laughter was heard when, in the year 1970, Pope Paul VI solemnly proclaimed St. Teresa of Avila—a Doctor of the Church!

The Pilgrim

The old soldier was shaking as he entered the box. He could not even remember how long it had been since his last confession. It was certainly more than twenty years, and he had a tale to tell which would surely bring yells of horror from the other side of the grille.

As he knelt down his knees shook. He wanted to turn and run. Why, why had he come? He knew why, of course. It was all because of the priest—this same one who now leaned forward to hear the long catalogue of his sins.

Through the grille the soldier could see the pale, aristocratic face half-turned from him; the thin, reddish hair and pointed beard. Yes, he looked infinitely wise and patient and kind, just as he had looked when he was up there in the pulpit, making everyone weep as he talked about the mercy of God which was waiting for everyone . . .

Well, it was no use running now. He was here and he would just have to get on with it. He began to stutter, then to panic. The words just wouldn't come.

With a half-raised hand and a quiet smile, the priest stopped him.

"My friend, you are embarrassed," he said. "No doubt

you are afraid that you will shock me. Well, perhaps if I tell you a little of my own early life, you will realise that I too am a sinner like yourself . . ."

Inigo's technique never failed. The most nervous penitent could not help but forget his own fears as he found himself listening to the confessor's sins before blurting out his own.

Like the man who now leaned forward, fascinated, Father Inigo Lopez de Loyola had himself been a soldier—a swashbuckling Basque knight in the army of Castile. Oh yes, there had been amorous adventures, but his besetting sin, Inigo recalled, was pride. Once, a group of rowdies had deliberately jostled him in the streets of Pamplona. He had run after them with his sword drawn, and if some passers-by had not grabbed him, he would certainly have run one of them through.

It was in Pamplona that he received his wound—the wound had left him with a permanent limp, the wound which had been the turning-point in his life. . . .

All the world knows the next part of the story: how Inigo, his leg shattered, was carried back to the family castle at Guipuzcoa; how he bore two torturing operations without flinching; how, while convalescing, he read some lives of the saints because there was nothing else to read and resolved that from now on, all his fighting would be done for God.

It was not a sudden conversion, for at that time Inigo was deeply attached to a beautiful young lady and his thoughts often wandered back in her direction. But he realised, after many months of being inwardly borne to and fro, that it was only the thought of God that brought him enduring peace and happiness.

In February, 1522, Ignatius—to give him his more familiar name—said farewell to his family and set off for the famous Benedictine Abbey of Montserrat, in northeast Spain. There he made a retreat in which he confessed all the sins of his past life—a task which took three days!

The laws of chivalry demanded that the young squire spend the whole night in prayer before donning the armor of full-fledged knighthood. Ignatius, who was now thirty, spent his night in prayer, but in the morning he put on no armor. Instead he hung his sword and dagger near Our Lady's statue as a votive offering, gave his fine clothes to a beggar and walked out of the church dressed in sack-cloth.

He was full of splendid ideals, but still far from sainthood—as we can judge from an incident on the journey to Montserrat. Riding along on his mule, Ignatius caught up with a Moor who, in the course of conversation, expressed doubt as to whether Our Lady could have remained a virgin after the birth of her Son. The poor man meant no disrespect; he was simply expressing an honestly-held view. But Ignatius thought quite seriously about killing him and would probably have done so had the Moor not galloped off in alarm. Even then, Ignatius thought about following him, but decided to leave the issue to the mule. Happily, God took the bridle and it chose a different road from the one taken by the terrified Moor.

His retreat at the abbey did not transform his character, but it did help Ignatius to identify his problem. When he took his leave of the monks, he knew that he had got to subdue the proud *hidalgo* in him, and he set about the task with terrifying vigor.

For the next eleven months, the little town of Manresa, near Barcelona, acquired a strange new citizen. For part of the time Ignatius lived in the local hospital, where he helped to tend the patients, and later in the Dominican house, where the kindly friars put a cell at his disposal. But much of his time was spent in a cave beside the River Cardoner, where he fasted, prayed and scourged

himself so severely that his Dominican hosts begged him
to stop.

He had always been vain about his appearance. Now,
like a desert father, he ceased to wash himself; his hair,
beard and nails were left to grow until his appearance
was frightening. In this state, the fine gentleman whose
home was a castle went about the streets begging his
bread.

And yet people seemed to·realise from the first that
there was something special about him. They began to
consult him about their spiritual problems and, when he
seemed utterly exhausted, they took him into their
homes and looked after him.

His sufferings at this time were not only physical. He
underwent the "dark night" described by so many mystics, when God seemed to have deserted him completely.
He was tortured by scruples, fearing that his every
thought, word and action were sinful.

One day, as he walked along the river bank to the
church outside the village, he had an experience so
wonderful that he could never afterwards put it properly
into words. There was no vision, but an inner illumina-
tion which enabled him to see things in a totally new
way. He understood truth so vividly and clearly that he
became, in his own words, "another man".

Soon afterwards he began work on a little book which
was to guide the lives of thousands of men—including
more than thirty canonised saints—and which still
provides the basic training of Jesuits throughout the
world:

> Just as walking, marching and running are bodily
> exercises, so the methods of preparing and disposing
> the soul . . . can be called the spiritual exercises.

The *Spiritual Exercises* often disappoint the reader who comes to them unprepared. The book itself is a small one: it can be read in a couple of hours. It has no pretensions to style; Ignatius never designed it as a piece of literature. It is a working manual, intended for use under the guidance of a spiritual director; a planned series of meditations for which the book itself is merely a framework.

Nevertheless, there are passages of profound grandeur:

Man is created to praise, reverence and serve God our Lord, and by this means to save his soul. The other things on the face of the earth are created for man's sake, to help him to pursue the end for which he is created. It follows, therefore, that a man must make use of them insofar as they help him to attain his end, and withdraw himself from them insofar as they hinder him. For this reason we must make ourselves indifferent to all created things, so far as we are permitted to do so and not forbidden. In other words, we should not prefer health to sickness, wealth to poverty, honor to dishonor, a long life to a short life. In all other things, likewise, we should desire and choose only those which most lead us to the end for which we are created.

The meditations, carried out over a period of four weeks, take the exercitant through the main events of Our Lord's life. By using his imagination, he is to place himself at the scene and to consider the meaning and the importance, especially to himself, of what happened there.

There are practical rules: on the use of food, for example; on the distribution of alms and on dealing with scruples! Daily examination of conscience is to become a lifelong practice.

Ignatius did not publish his *Spiritual Exercises* for many years, but by the time he left Manresa, he had the fundamentals worked out. Unlike earlier techniques, which were designed for religious living in community, this one was clearly designed for people living in the world—including lay people. The emphasis was on the individual: God was to be sought everywhere and in everything, in all the ordinary affairs of life.

Throughout his autobiography, which he dictated towards the end of his life, Ignatius refers to himself in the third person, as "The Pilgrim". In March, 1523, he became a real pilgrim, heading for Jerusalem with his precious manuscript in his meagre pack.

He did not yet have any precise idea of his mission in life. In the Holy Land, he believed that he had found it. He would make his home there and work for the conversion of the Moslems.

The Franciscan priests who looked after the Holy Places swiftly scotched that idea. Relations with the Moslems were always fraught with tension, and this eccentric fellow was just the kind of man who could spell trouble. Why, even on the voyage over, the sailors had threatened to dump him on a desert island after he berated them for their filthy conduct!

"After the Pilgrim had learned that God did not wish him to stay in Jerusalem, he pondered in his heart what he ought to do. He decided to study for a time in order that he might be able to help souls." In those words Ignatius himself describes his next move.

His studies, which lasted for more than twelve years, began in Barcelona. There, the 33-year-old aristocrat sat humbly on a bench beside mischievous little schoolboys, learning to decline *mensa* and to conjugate *amo*. When thoughts of God came to his mind during lesson-time, he brushed them aside. Latin grammar was the task in hand and Latin grammar it was going to be. He even asked the master to whack him if he were found inattentive— though whether this was ever done is not recorded!

Replete with declensions and conjugations, Ignatius eventually said good-bye to Barcelona and his tittering schoolfellows, and set out on a 400-mile trek to the great University of Alcala, not far from Madrid.

Here, as everywhere he went, Ignatius lost no opportunity of talking to people about the spiritual life; trying out on them the ideas which he had written out so carefully in that manuscript in his knapsack. Soon he had a regular group of friends, all imbued with his ideas and eager to imitate his mode of life. They even imitated his style of dress—the sack-cloth habit and the hood that went with it.

For a layman to form any kind of religious association, however loose and informal, was asking for trouble. One bright morning, Ignatius found himself a prisoner of the Inquisition.

It was not a very rigorous imprisonment; while he was inside, Ignatius went right on seeing his friends and giving his spiritual exercises. Eventually he was summoned before the Inquisitor and told that he had been cleared of heresy, but that he and his friends must not discuss religion with anyone until they had completed three years of study, and only then with official permission. Also, they must abandon their "habit" and dress like everyone else. Learning that they could not afford new clothes, the kindly Inquisitor gave them money from his own pocket.

To escape the restrictions, Ignatius and his friends moved on to Salamanca, where again they swifly found themselves in trouble. This time the imprisonment—in the Bishop's official jail—was more severe; they were chained together in a rat-infested cell. The "sentence" was the same as before: not guilty of heresy, but no more teaching—or else!

At this point, Ignatius decided that Spain was too hot to hold him. Bidding farewell to his companions, he set out alone for the University of Paris.

Spain, as it happened, was then at war with France, but Ignatius did not let that worry him. He arrived in Paris on February 2nd, 1528, and began the incredibly spartan life of a theology student, rising at four in the morning, attending lectures until six or seven in the evening, and all on a starvation diet.

The hardships did not worry him, for he was well used to them, but he was sorry for those who suffered and often distributed money that he had begged.

One of those whom he helped was an elegant young cleric called Francis Xavier, a Basque aristocrat like himself, but a worldly fellow with his eye fixed firmly on the ladder of ecclesiastical preferment. Francis was actually an instructor in logic, but a very impoverished one. At first he took a poor view of his limping compatriot, who let the side down by begging in the streets. But Ignatius won him over, and Francis was soon to become one of the first Jesuits and one of the greatest Jesuit saints.

For once again, Ignatius was gathering round himself a group of devoted companions and, although none of them yet knew it, they were to form the nucleus of the new Society of Jesus.

At dawn on the Feast of the Assumption, August 15th, 1534, Ignatius and six of his friends got up at sunrise and walked to a little chapel on Montmartre. One of the group, Peter Favre, was already a priest, and he said Mass. At the Communion, the six men in the little congregation each took three vows: poverty, chastity, and a vow to travel to Palestine and spend their lives working there. Peter did not take the vow of chastity, for he had taken it already, but he took the other two. Mass over, the group picnicked happily together and discussed plans for their journey.

They never did get to Palestine; the war between Venice and the Turks made it impossible to get a boat. So they fell back on their alternative plan, to present themselves to Pope Paul III for any work which he might choose to give them.

The Pope, impressed, gave them permission to be ordained and assigned them to various tasks. Ignatius he asked to give the spiritual exercises in and around Rome. On June 24th, 1537, the former warrior was ordained priest, along with most of his companions, in the Italian town of Vicenza.

Soon afterwards he had a vision in which Our Lord told him: "My will is that you should serve us." In 1539, he and his companions formed themselves into a permanent society. The Society of Jesus had been born.

Soon afterwards he had a vision in which Our Lord told him: "My will is that you should serve us." In 1539, he and his companions formed themselves into a permanent society. The Society of Jesus had been born.

From the very outset, the new organisation attracted suspicion and hostility—inside the Church, as well as outside. Who had ever heard of a religious order which wore no distinctive habit, which did not sing office in choir, and whose members were prepared to go anywhere and do anything at the Pope's behest?

Dominic had realised the need for mobility; Ignatius carried it to its logical conclusion. He broke with the old monastic forms altogether and provided the Church with a new and trained army, equipped to fight the Church's battles on all fronts.

Obedience is the first characteristic of the soldier, and

so it was with the army of Ignatius. His men took a special vow of obedience to the Pope which was, in the
words of their founder, "the cause and principal foundation of his society". He himself set out the ideal in a
letter which he wrote to all of them during those first
years:

> I must not belong to myself at all, but to my Creator
> and to His vicar. I must be like a ball of wax, ready to
> be directed and moved about just as it allows itself
> to be kneaded . . . I must be like a corpse, without
> will or understanding; like a tiny crucifix, which is
> moved about without resisting; like a staff in the
> hand of an old man, to be placed wherever he wishes
> and can use it best.

This came as a clarion-call to young men, who flocked
to the colors in their hundreds. By the time Ignatius died
there were a thousand Jesuits at work all over the world.
Francis Xavier had gone to the Far East, where he was to
die alone in a hut at the very gates of China. Elsewhere,
Jesuits were running missions in the Congo, in Ethiopia,
in South America, in Protestant England.

Ignatius had at first been reluctant to get involved in
education, but soon he recognised its importance and
here, too, his order became a major force. In Rome itself
he founded the college which became the embryo of the
Gregorian university, and the German College which
still flourishes today. There was scarcely any branch of
learning, or any other field of activity, in which Jesuits
did not involve themselves, in the words of their motto,
"for the greater glory of God".

Over this dramatic growth Ignatius presided, not
willingly, for he had told his first members that he did
not wish to rule. But they elected him just the same, and

he celebrated his appointment by sending himself to work in the kitchen!

Throughout his reign, Ignatius was dogged by ill-health; yet again and again he recovered and went back to work, tireless as ever. On July 30th, 1566, knowing that this time his end was near, he asked his secretary to go to the Pope and ask for his last blessing.

The secretary, Father Polanco, could not believe that Ignatius was really dying. After all, he had been ill fifteen times in as many years. Anxious to catch next day's overseas mail, the secretary asked if he might delay the errand so that he could finish his letters. He would go to the Pope tomorrow.

"The sooner you go, the happier I will be," replied Ignatius. "However, do as you wish."

Tomorrow was too late, as it so often is. At daybreak on July 31st, Ignatius Loyola died, alone and without the Last Sacraments.

Rome's Laughing
Apostle

It was not a very respectful way for a bunch of little urchins to greet a priest. "Here he comes," they yelled delightedly. "Here comes old Philip!"

Philip Neri saw them and laughed. The young men with him laughed, even the red-faced one who had been made to carry his plump white dog. Everywhere Philip went, people laughed.

What a sight he looked, walking at the head of his friends in his ridiculous white shoes, laughing and singing, sniffing at a bunch of prickly broom as though it were some gorgeous bouquet. And there was no end to the mad things he did. Why, once he had even shaved half his beard off, leaving world-weary Romans, who thought they had seen everything, to goggle after him as he sported the other half through the streets of the Eternal City.

Yet Philip was not mad, as those who joined his merry band quickly discovered. Catherine of Siena and Teresa of Avila loved gaiety, and used it to help others to get to Heaven. Philip's antics served the same purpose, but he went a stage further. He became a buffoon.

Born in Florence, he was eighteen when he left home to work for a relative who had a business near Naples.

But a merchant's life was not for Philip as anyone who knew him well might have guessed. For even as a small child, his mind had been fixed on God. It was said that in his early years he only committed one sin—when he gave his sister an impatient push because she interrupted his singing of the psalms. To his family and friends he was always *Pippo Buono*—"Good little Phil".

After only a few months in his cousin's counting-house, Philip made for Rome, without any plans or visible means of support. Possibly he did not even intend to stay, but stay he did for the rest of his long life—a life that spanned most of the sixteenth century.

Rome had a sizable Florentine community and it was with one of these, a customs official called Galeotto Caccia, that the young man found a home. In return for an attic room and the bare necessities of life, he acted as tutor to Galeotto's two small sons.

We would give much to know how Philip got along with his two charges, Michele and Ippolito. We have their mother's assurance that under Philip's care they became "two little angels", but no information on how the miracle was achieved.

Up there in his little garret Philip lived more frugally than many a monk. He ate only bread, olives and salad, with an egg now and again, and meat hardly ever. He often drank water instead of wine—very unusual in Italy! His only furniture was a bed, a chair, a few books and a line on which he hung his clothes.

Apart from the time he spent with the boys he lived as a recluse, keeping to his room and often passing whole nights in prayer.

His long retreat lasted for two years: when he emerged, it was to take college courses in philosophy and theology, though there is no evidence that he had any intention of becoming a priest or of entering a religious order.

In one of the colleges Philip attended, Sant' Agostino, there was a large crucifix. Whenever he saw it, he often used to weep. It was not simply the thought of Christ's passion and death that brought the tears to his eyes, but the cynical neglect that He was suffering here in the so-called centre of Christendom.

For, with all its lip-service to the Master, Renaissance Rome was a pagan city—a city where prelates found it boring to say Mass when they might be lining their pockets; where the learned read Homer rather than the Bible; where courtesans catered for cardinals and an illegitimate family was no bar to a man's election as Pope. Perhaps we should not be surprised that God sent a humble layman to be its apostle.

"Well, brothers, and when shall we begin to do good?" With this simple, artless question, Philip began his sixty-year mission among the baptised pagans of the Eternal City. Even from a priest or a religious, the question would have come as a surprise. To the young Florentines, lounging during their lunch-hour among the shops and banks where they worked, it was positively startling to have someone of their own age, a fellow-exile from Florence, challenge them with it on a street-corner.

Soon it ceased to startle them; they came to expect it as they came to expect Philip, regular as clockwork, always with the same friendly smile and the same friendly greeting. Soon it became as familiar as a television comic's catchphrase. "Well, brothers, and when shall we begin to do good?"

Before long many did begin to do good. They came with Philip to visit the sick in the horrifying hospitals; they came with him to pray in the Seven Churches—a devotion which Philip began and which endures to this day.

He founded a lay confraternity which looked after poor

pilgrims: from it sprang a great hostel, Santa Trinità dei Pelligrini, which cared for many thousands of pilgrims and, later, poor convalescents.

After three years of college, he had now abandoned his studies. At last he had found his vocation.

The number of his followers grew steadily, but always, with the evening, he would go off somewhere to pray alone. Sometimes he would make his night-long prayers in a church porch, but often he would go to the catacombs of St. Sebastian, to pray at the tombs of the first martyrs.

It was in the catacombs, on the eve of Pentecost in 1544, that Philip suddenly saw above him a globe of fire. Slowly it came towards him and—to his own astonishment—entered his mouth. Once inside him, it seemed to dilate, and at the same time he felt such an intensity of divine love that he felt sure he must die of it. Rolling on the ground he begged God to spare him: "No more, Lord, no more—I am only a poor mortal man."

Soon he rose, feeling more calm. He put his hand to his heart, and discovered a swelling about the size of a man's fist. It remained there until the day of his death, more than fifty years later. Never once did he feel pain from it, yet a post-mortem revealed that two of his ribs had been broken.

In later years, when he was a priest and hearing confessions, he would often press the penitent's head to this place above his heart. Just by doing this, he could bring happiness and peace flooding into another's soul, so that no one who had the experience ever forgot it.

Many other strange things began to happen, too, after that memorable Whitsun. Philip's body-heat, for example, often rose well above normal, so that he could not bear to be indoors and found the weight of his shirt oppressive, even in winter.

Even when he was elderly, he would go bare-chested, on the coldest nights, up on to the roof. When the young men remonstrated he would laugh and invite them to feel his skin, which glowed as though he were sunburned.

Some of the other phenomena he found less laughable: in particular, the trembling which so often shook him, especially when he said Mass. In vain did he press his elbows against the altar in an effort to control it; the trembling remained plainly visible to all. Sometimes his body swelled and some thought that he levitated, his feet rising from the floor.

Very frequently, he would go into an ecstatic trance, so that the server would leave him after the Communion, putting a notice on the door to say that Father Philip was inside. Two hours later he would return and Mass would proceed normally.

Philip's constant clowning was, we can be certain, his way of distracting people's attention from these events, for he hated to think that anyone might regard him as a saint. Yet there was scarcely one of his friends who did not so regard him. His confessor, Father Persiano Rossa actually called him "Saint Philip".

He was thirty-five when he was finally ordained, and even then it needed a great deal of persuasion from Father Rossa. Ever afterwards, Philip insisted that he had taken the step purely out of obedience to his confessor. Left to himself, he would have remained as he was.

Soon he was the most popular man in Rome. People flocked to him. Invited to choose either Philip or the Pope as their confessor, most would have chosen Philip without a moment's hesitation—despite the strange and wonderful penances that he was apt to impose!

Was a young man too self-important, a little too conscious of his own dignity? Philip sent him out in a Roman midsummer, wearing a heavy fur coat—and the more people who stared at him, the better the confessor was pleased.

A young lady, sent to help at a local orphanage, came back wrinkling her nose at the lice that crept about in the poor children's beds.

"Go back and eat one!" Philip commanded.

"Father, you can't be serious!" the horrified young woman gasped.

"Go back and do as I say!"

There was no arguing with him, she knew that. Trembling, she returned to her bedmaking. The beds were as filthy as ever, but there was not a louse to be seen, though they had been legion a short time before.

"Well?" demanded Philip, when she returned.

Nervous and bewildered, she told him the truth—that she had failed to find a louse.

Philip said nothing. As she recalled afterwards, he just smiled a little smile.

Perhaps this penance had a double purpose, for, like so many other saints, Philip loved all God's creatures, lice no doubt included. A lifelong vegetarian, he was deeply distressed when, during his old age, doctors forced him to eat meat for his health. "It won't do me any good," he declared. And it did not.

One of his greatest friends was the dog Capriccio, who has already appeared in this narrative. Originally he belonged to Cardinal Sforza, one of Rome's grandest prelates, but one day he followed a friend of Philip's to San Girolamo, the church where he lived. From that moment he forsook his distinguished master for good. No matter how often he was returned to His Eminence's palace, he always came trotting back to Philip's humble room.

Some of the Cardinal's household had joined Philip's circle and the Cardinal was not pleased. "He's taken my men away," he grumbled, "and now he's taken my dog."

Along with St. Teresa, Philip could not stand sullen

saints, and solemnity he treated as though it were a vice. Caesar Baronius, who himself became a cardinal and a distinguished historian, was made to sing the *"Miserere"* at a wedding to cure him of this lamentable fault. In Philip's eyes, any form of holiness which did not leave room for laughter was gravely suspect.

Great ceremonies he disliked and did not trouble to hide the fact. Once, during a papal procession, he dashed forward and tugged at a Swiss Guard's beard! This showed what Philip thought of the procession; what the guard thought of Philip we have, perhaps fortunately, not been told.

Philip spoke to everyone, even cardinals, in a friendly fashion. Such titles as "Eminence" and "Excellency" did not exist as far as he was concerned, and instead of the formal second-person *Lei,* he used the more familiar *voi* when addressing important persons.

He spent many hours a day in the confessional, and often knew a penitent's secrets before they were told. Sometimes, if a young man had sinned against the sixth commandment, he kept away from Philip and went elsewhere to confession. But next time he came, Philip always knew what had happened. "You stink!" he would shout disgustedly.

But if Philip could be blunt, he could also be gentle; for he could read troubles, as well as sins, without being told. And he often consoled people simply with a look, so that no words were spoken at all.

When his little room at the Church of San Girolamo became too small to hold the crowd of visitors, a loft over the nave was converted into a chapel without an altar— an oratory. With the help of other priests Philip held regular conferences there, ringing a little bell as a general invitation. Very soon, the regular attenders got a nickname, "Oratorians".

These Oratory sessions were democratic in the

extreme—remarkably so for that time. Priests and layfolk sat together on benches, holding discussions in which anyone might join. There were readings, prayers and hymns, together with a set sermon. It all took about three hours and the Oratorians could come and go as they liked. This informality was another refreshing feature.

Philip did not dominate the proceedings; he spoke remarkably little. Instead, he helped others to give the best they had in them.

Sometimes the Oratorians listened to the letters of the first Jesuit missionaries, who were just beginning their work in the mission countries. St. Francis Xavier, especially, fired Philip's imagination. He began to have doubts about the work he was doing: should he really be here in the safety of Rome, when millions in far-off lands had never even heard the name of Christ?

He put his problem to a wise and holy Cistercian. The reply was terse: "Rome must be your Indies." From then on, Philip had no more doubts.

Though his Oratory had been founded for laymen, inevitably it produced vocations to the priesthood. Within a few years, Philip was presenting five candidates for ordination.

Had he now founded a religious order? No, he had not! Philip steadfastly refused to take vows, or to allow his Oratorians to do so. They must, he insisted, live together freely, without canonical ties of any kind. The only bond must be the bond of love. To this day, the priests and lay-brothers of the Oratories around the world are organised on the same principle. Each house is independent of the rest, and its members, still, take no vows.

If any of his young friends wanted to join a religious order, or if they appeared to have that kind of vocation, Philip sent them off with his blessing. Ignatius Loyola—whom Philip knew and admired—received many recruits from him. Indeed, Ignatius himself described Philip as a bell ringing outside his Society, inviting others to come in but never entering himself. Evidently Ignatius would dearly have loved to make a Jesuit out of Philip!

Like Ignatius, Philip more than once came under suspicion of heresy and was in fact investigated by the Inquisition without actually being arrested. The two Dominicans entrusted with the task sent back glowing reports—which was hardly surprising, since they had both known Philip since they were youngsters.

Despite this, the saintly Pope Pius VI pronounced himself still worried about the role which Philip gave to laymen; to him it all seemed very Protestant. But he took no further action and the Oratory flourished.

Towards the end of his life, Philip was the dearly-loved friend of two Popes, Gregory XIV and Clement VIII. Gregory was an indecisive man and Philip chided him for this fault. Clement he once cured of gout simply by shaking hands with him—though the Pope, in great pain, yelled in alarm and begged him not to try. It was simply one of the many cures which Philip performed during his long life.

Early on May 26th, 1595, Philip himself became gravely ill. To a friend who went into his room, he announced: "I'm on my way." Soon afterwards, very peacefully, he died.

By planting himself as a missionary at the heart of the Church, and making worldly men holy, Philip exercised an influence which cannot be calculated. He contributed greatly to the success of the Counter-Reformation.

Today his sons exercise an influence out of proportion to their numbers, just as they have always done. When the great Cardinal John Henry Newman became a Catholic and a priest, it was Philip's family that he chose to join.

The Grand Inquisitor

"The Pope will be named on Monday," Philip Neri prophesied. Asked who it would be, he was reluctant at first to name him. Eventually he did so and was, of course, swiftly proved right. On Monday, January 7th, 1566, Cardinal Michael Ghislieri became Pope Pius V.

The fun-loving people of Rome liked their popes to be worldly men like themselves, not too holy, and tolerant of human weakness. From their point of view, the Sacred College could hardly have made a worse choice.

From the day of his coronation, it was obvious that Pope Pius was going to be very different from most of his Renaissance predecessors. This time there were no handfuls of cash from the papal coffers scattered to the Roman crowds; no sumptuous banquet for cardinals and ambassadors. Instead the money went to hospitals and the poor.

Unlike those other, less worthy occupants of Peter's throne, the new Pope had had a humble start in life. The Ghislieri family lived at Bosco, in Northern Italy. They had been aristocrats, but by the time little Antonio came along on June 13th, 1504, they had gone down in the world—so much so that the future pontiff was sent to work as a shepherd-boy to earn a little money.

He took the name Michael when, at the age of fourteen, he joined the Dominicans at Vigevano, near Milan. A rich neighbour, who recognised his talent, had paid for his earlier schooling. Soon he was one of the order's shining lights, first as a professor and later as novice-master.

His next appointment was with the Inquisition. There is no way of making that statement without its sounding sinister. Yet Michael, like many other inquisitors, did his work honestly and fairly. His job was to protect people from ideas which threatened both their immortal souls and the peace and order of their day-to-day lives.

One of the most spirited modern defences of the Inquisition was made by—of all people—the late George Bernard Shaw. In the preface to *St. Joan,* he argued that, given the conditions of the time, the Inquisition was a necessary institution and that it operated a much better system of justice than most secular courts. Indeed, said Shaw, the average Inquisition hearing was much fairer to the accused than a British field court-martial!

Nevertheless, inquisitors were not popular people and on at least one occasion Michael was physically attacked (another Dominican Inquisitor, St. Peter Martyr, was assassinated). This did not stop him from pressing ahead fearlessly, even when those whom he investigated were people of power and influence.

An appeal against the confiscation of some heretical books was taken to Rome, where Michael won his case so skillfully that he impressed the powerful Cardinal Caraffa. On Caraffa's recommendation, he was transferred to Rome as the Inquisition's commissary-general—the top man.

Caraffa became Pope Paul IV; Michael became a bishop and, very quickly, a cardinal. "The Holy Father has fastened irons to my feet to stop me from creeping back to the cloister," he observed ruefully, from which we can deduce that he preferred life as a simple friar to the high-powered life of the Roman curia.

In the years that followed, he must often have wished himself back with his Dominican novices, for Pope Paul proved to be a morose and irascible man, given to issuing haughty edicts which could only lead to trouble. Michael, one of the few people the Pope would listen to, managed to modify some of his worst excesses.

The next Pope, Pius IV, was a complete contrast. A member of the renowned Medici family, he was far too worldly for Michael to tolerate quietly, and when he tried to make a 13-year-old relative a cardinal, Michael spoke out boldly. To his credit, Pius did not hold it against him, nor did he when Michael again criticised him for attempting to subsidise a nephew out of papal funds.

It was inevitable that the Dominican cardinal's qualities would bring him many admirers. By far the most important of these was St. Charles Borromeo, Archbishop of Milan and one of the great leaders of the Counter-Reformation. Like Michael himself, he lived a life of extreme austerity amid the trappings of ecclesiastical splendor, eating and sleeping little and spending long hours in prayer. Charles visited every one of the 1,000 parishes in his archdiocese, ministered personally to the stricken during a plague outbreak and sold the furnishings from his palace to give money to the poor.

When the Throne of Peter once more became vacant, it was Charles who saw to it that the choice fell on Michael Ghislieri.

And so, after the long play-time of the Renaissance, Rome found itself with a saint for a ruler—not a jolly saint, like Philip Neri, but a puritan who forbade priests to visit taverns or theatres, banned bull-fights, drove all the prostitutes out of the city and was only with difficulty dissuaded from making adultery a capital offence.

"He's trying to turn Rome into a monastery," sneered the worldly, but they were wrong. To promote virtue and eradicate vice was clearly the duty of any Pope, and in an age when he had the political and legislative means at his disposal, it was natural that he should use them to enforce his reforms.

That reforms were desperately needed, no one could deny. Protestantism was sweeping through Europe; the Moslem hordes were threatening to make the Mediterranean a Turkish lake. Pius V, facing these two terrible threats, knew that his first task was to stamp out the corruption and the moral softness which had come with the Renaissance, and to recall Catholics to their ideals.

Philip Neri did the same thing from the opposite end: he worked personally, among individuals. Pius V, because he was Pope, operated on a larger scale. He did not concern himself only with the sins of ordinary folk: he reformed the Roman curia and stamped down on nepotism and the other abuses which he had fought as a cardinal.

Towards heretics he was strict, yet he was no bloodthirsty sadist. The cruelty of the Spanish Inquisition—which had become a tool of the State—appalled him and he did his utmost to prevent it. When Bartolomé Carranza, the Dominican Archbishop of Toledo, was falsely accused of heresy, Pius had him brought to Rome, where he was finally acquitted.

Perhaps it was inevitable that, in the atmosphere that he created, someone so highly individual as Philip Neri should have been suspected of Protestantism. Yet when the Pope died, Philip begged some of his clothes from the master of the papal wardrobe and kept them as relics of a man whom he had long regarded as a saint.

By that time many others had come to the same conclusion: hostility had been transmuted into veneration. For, strict though he was, austere though he was, the holy old Dominican was hardest of all on himself.

Throughout his pontificate he suffered badly from stones, yet he wore a hairshirt under his robes, hardly ate anything, and never stopped working. Like Pope John XXIII he preferred walking to riding, he never let himself or anyone else forget his humble origins, and he visited the seven churches of Rome on foot.

Despite the cares of his office, he found time to visit the sick and, sometimes, to care for them personally. When famine hit Rome, he organised a relief system that would have done credit to Gregory the Great. At his own expense he imported large quantities of corn from France and Sicily and either gave it away or sold it at less than cost price.

Even in his appearance, Pius V inspired reverence and awe. He looked every inch a saint, and it is said that an English Protestant was converted to Catholicism simply by looking at him.

Yet, with all his great virtues, he made a fundamental mistake: he constantly confused his own spiritual authority as Pope with his ordinary authority as a temporal ruler. He believed that he could over-ride other sovereigns politically whenever he chose to do so, and that Catholics everywhere owed political allegiance to him.

Pius V was not the first Pope to think in this misguided fashion, nor the last. But he brought disaster upon English Catholics by excommunicating Queen Elizabeth 1, encouraging Spain to make war against England, and releasing the Queen's Catholic subjects from their allegiance to her. Most of them were loyal to Elizabeth and had no love for Spain, yet by his inept action the Pope put them in the position of traitors and gave her every excuse for persecuting them.

In dealing with the Turkish menace, Pius was much more successful. In May, 1571, he signed an alliance between the Holy See, Spain and the Venetian Republic.

On October 7th, a combined fleet under Don John of Austria defeated the Turks at Lepanto, effectively crushing their sea-power once and for all.

On the day of the battle Pius ordered prayers to be said in all Rome's churches, and the story goes that during the evening, as he was holding a conference with some cardinals, he suddenly rose from the table, went to a window and opened it, and stood gazing out across Rome.

Then he closed the window, turned to the cardinals and told them: "This is no time to be talking business together. Instead let us thank God for the victory which he has granted to the arms of Christ!"

Not for several days did news of Don John's success reach Rome. Seven months later, Pope Pius was dead.

Today Pius V is mainly remembered as the Pope who imposed the Tridentine Mass on the Western Church. Prior to his decree, in July, 1570, Mass had been said in a variety of forms. Pius considered that uniformity would help to ensure that the Holy Sacrifice was always celebrated properly and that superstition and other abuses were stamped out.

In the midst of our present-day controversies, it may be useful to reflect that in its day, the Tridentine Mass was itself an innovation unwelcome to many! There was much nostalgia for the older forms—the English Sarum rite, for example, which it replaced.

Yet by no means all his achievements were negative. If Pius was a puritan he was also an Italian—a lover of painting and of music. He gave his patronage to several gifted artists, but above all to the composer Palestrina, who got his big chance in life when Pius made him master of the papal chapel. It was Pius V, too, who sponsored the first major edition of Thomas Aquinas's works, and who proclaimed him a Doctor of the Church.

It would certainly have surprised him to learn that he

would one day be regarded as the patron saint of conservatives. For Pius was, above all, a reformer. In cracking down on corruption, re-shaping the liturgy, and making the clergy do their jobs properly, he was disturbing the comfortable norms of his time.

He reigned for only six years. Throughout that time he strove tirelessly to enforce the controversial new measures laid down by the 18-year-long Council of Trent. And he succeeded.

Yet it took the Church some time to recognise his greatness. Four other great saints of the Renaissance—Teresa of Avila, Ignatius Loyola, Francis Xavier and Philip Neri—were all canonised on the same day in 1622. But it was not until 1712 that Pius V, also, was proclaimed a saint.

Red Cross Saint

Visiting a large English hospital some years ago, I found myself in conversation with the senior male nurse, a dour Lancashire man. I happened to mention the name of Florence Nightingale, with what I hoped was due reverence. The response was unexpected.

"I suppose you think," the nurse said drily, "that she more or less founded our profession."

I admitted that I had been under that impression.

"Well, she didn't," he declared. "*He* did."

He pointed to a statue, high in the wall. The figure of a priest, a red cross shining from his black cassock, watched over the double row of cheerful patients.

Camillus de Lellis—I recognised him, of course, though not until much later did I realise how good a claim he has to be called the father of scientific nursing. Yet, amazingly, many who have devoted their lives to the sick have never heard of him; and more than one history of nursing has been published without mention of his name.

Camillus was born in the little hill-town of Bucchianico, in the Abruzzi, on May 25th, 1550; more than 300 years before Florence Nightingale set out for the Crimea. His mother, the wife of a minor nobleman, was nearly sixty when she found that a new baby was on the way.

Shortly before the birth, she dreamed that she saw her baby, signed with a cross, followed by a great company of other children similarly signed. The omen might have delighted her, but Donna Camilla was not an optimist. She decided that she was about to give birth to a bandit.

However, she was a devout woman and when labour began, she hurried from the church where she was hearing Mass to a place nearby where horses were kept. Camillus, like Jesus, was born in a stable.

The infant was abnormally large—he grew up to be 6 feet 6 inches tall and broad in proportion. His father danced for joy. "We must send him to school at once!" he roared.

Unfortunately, his enthusiasm did not suffice to make him a good father. He was often away at the wars, and Camillus grew up wild and undisciplined; in our day, he would certainly have ended in the children's court. He frequently ran away from school, no tutor could manage him, and he inherited his father's hot temper and his passion for gambling.

In 1567, when Camillus was 17, his father once again went off to fight the Turks; but this time he took his boy with him. Two young cousins went along too.

But they never saw the Turks. At Luchino, near Loreto, they were caught in a fever epidemic. Within a few weeks old Giovanni de Lellis was dead. Camillus, broken-hearted, lay shaking and sweating for weeks. A terrible sore opened on his right foot.

When he was well enough to move, he set out sadly for home. On the dusty road he caught sight of two Franciscans and their gentle faces, serene in their poverty, caught at his heart. Then and there Camillus made up his mind: no more fighting and no more gambling. He, too, would follow St. Francis.

A wise old friar heard his story, heard him offer his life to the order. He shook his head. Camillus, he felt sure, was simply running away from his troubles: seeking in religion a refuge from illness and depression.

The sore on his foot was no better; indeed, it was growing worse. So Camillus set out for Rome and the Hospital of San Giacomo. He arrived there early in March, 1571, and by the end of the month the foot seemed to be healed.

However, he did not leave the hospital but stayed on to work as an attendant at a monthly salary of about fourteen cents. No doubt he was glad of the job; though nobly born, he was miserably poor. A sword and a cloak were all that his father had left to him by way of legacy.

The conditions in which Camillus worked were horrifying in the extreme. San Giacomo, like many hospitals of the time, was a foul and stinking den of misery where helpless patients were frequently left in unchanged beds to rot in their own filth. If they were fractious, the attendants beat them. Sometimes, unconscious patients were hurried to the morgue before they were dead.

Of course we are shocked, but we ought to remember that even in our gleaming, sanitised hospitals, carelessness and even brutality are not altogether unknown. Unfortunately, not everyone who cares for the sick has the exceptional qualities which the work requires.

Some of Camillus' colleagues were simply lazy or ignorant, some were vicious—discharged criminals who could not find any other employment. A few, a very few, were kind and dedicated, but they could not hope to beat the system or even to improve it.

In these surroundings, Camillus soon took up his old way of life. He quarreled, he fought and he gambled:

something strictly forbidden by hospital rules. By this time, his gambling was compulsive.

The hospital authorities, used though they were to rough and brutal men, found Camillus more than they could handle. His fights were disrupting the hospital; he was neglecting his patients to play cards with the Tiber boatmen. After nine months, Camillus was fired.

With no other job in sight, he joined the Venetian army just in time for a new war against the Turks. This time he saw active service in Greece and Yugoslavia: he took part in the assault on Barbagno, when the starving Christian forces cut the livers from Turkish bodies and ate them. Camillus, unable to face the cannibalism, survived on grass and horseflesh. In the army, also, his gambling got him into trouble: he was about to fight a duel when a sergeant-major stepped in and put a stop to it.

In May, 1573, Venice unexpectedly made peace with the Turks. Camillus now joined up with the Spaniards, gambling his way to Sicily and North Africa. At one game, in Naples, he lost literally everything, including the proverbial shirt. In later years, local mothers made a shrine of the spot where the game took place, praying there for their own erring sons.

During a stormy voyage back to Palermo, the terrified young soldier remembered his earlier ambition to become a Franciscan and vowed that if he were saved, he would indeed join the order. Back on dry land the promise was swiftly forgotten. Camillus resumed his old ways.

Demobilised once more, he wandered north to Manfredonia. Finally, penniless and starving, the young aristocrat was reduced to begging at a church door. One of the local gentry, moved to pity, offered to get him work with the Capuchins, who were building a new friary.

While children mocked his tattered uniform, Camillus toiled in the Italian sun, driving two mules loaded with stones, water and lime. Though the work was hard, he was happier than he had been for a long time. There were stormy moments: once he walked out because the friars would not give him a day off. They soon persuaded him to come back. When the building was finished, they let him stay on as a general handyman.

One day, Camillus was sent to another Capuchin friary, some miles distant, to buy wine. Something about the huge messenger must have impressed the Guardian there, for he took him to one side and spoke to him earnestly about the service of God and the salvation of his soul. He gave him some advice: "Whenever you have evil thoughts, spit in the devil's face."

Camillus set out again for Manfredonia, pondering all that the Guardian had said to him. Suddenly, his soul broken, he flung himself from the mule's back onto the hard ground. It was the Feast of Our Lady's Purification, February 2nd, 1575.

Back at his own friary, he begged the startled Guardian to receive him into the Capuchins. The Guardian said that he would have to ask permission. Camillus, while waiting for the outcome, undertook severe penances with all the enthusiasm which he had formerly devoted to card-games.

Permission granted, he was sent to Trivento to begin his novitiate. There, the once-quarrelsome aristocrat so distinguished himself by the meekness of his disposition that he became known as *il frate umile*, "the humble brother".

But Camillus was not to remain a Capuchin for long. The ulcerated foot had never properly healed; now, it suddenly grew worse. Within a few months he was forced to leave.

So it was that the Holy Year of 1575 found Camillus once again at the door of San Giacomo Hospital. The officials must have been astonished to see him, and even more astonished at the change in him.

Again the cure seemed to be successful and again Camillus stayed on as a staff member. This time, though, there was no fighting or gambling and soon Camillus was renowned for his hard work and his loving care of the patients. He was promoted to infirmarian, in charge of other attendants; then to hospital bursar.

At this time he acquired a new spiritual director, one whom we have already met: Philip Neri. "I, who have been so great a sinner, need a great saint," he declared.

Philip heard Camillus's confession weekly and allowed him to receive Holy Communion on all Sundays and feast-days, a rare privilege in those days. Evidently, Philip recognised that here was a saint in the making.

Not that the two always saw eye to eye. Against Philip's advice, Camillus insisted on returning to the Capuchins, but once again, his stay was short. His wound opened up again, just as Philip had said it would.

Convinced now that God wanted him to devote his life to the sick, Camillus returned for a third time to San Giacomo, became superintendent of the hospital, and set himself to fight the abuses.

He proved to be an astute businessman and a capable administrator. In the hospital he was here, there and everywhere. After he himself had rescued a living patient from the morgue, he ordered that the face should be left uncovered for at least fifteen minutes after apparent death so that the risk of mistake would be minimised. Well ahead of his time, he insisted on proper sanitary arrangements.

The spiritual care of the patients was his special concern. Here, too, there was much that desperately needed to be put right. Patients were regularly forced to make their confession on admission, even when they were semi-conscious. Priests, terrified of infection, rushed round giving Holy Communion to patients who immediately vomited back the Host.

Camillus could be tough: the worst of the attendants were fired just as he himself had been. Yet with the patients this big, forceful man was all tenderness. He washed, fed and deloused them, cheerfully and without a flicker of revulsion.

His reputation for holiness began to spread beyond the hospital walls. Regularly the Jesuits sent their novices to him for the hospital work that was part of their training. Their novice-master declared: "When they are in the hands of Signor Camillus I put my faith in him and remain at home."

Already Camillus and some of his more devout helpers were meeting for prayer before a crucifix in his room. It was now that he began to form the idea of a religious congregation devoted to the care of the sick.

Inevitably, there was suspicion and hostility, even before his great plan had declared itself. Why were they meeting in a room, the hospital authorities demanded. Were there not churches enough in Rome?

To allay criticism, the little group met in the hospital church instead. Camillus, in his sleep, received encouragement from the Figure on the crucifix: "Do not be afraid, O man of small soul. Go ahead, for I will encourage you and be with you."

On the Feast of the Assumption, 1582, the group took their first vows.

So far, they were all laymen. But if they were to care also for their patients' spiritual welfare, should not some of them, at least, be priests? The question was urgent and had to be faced.

Camillus knew very well that he was not nearly learned enough to be ordained: his general education had been sketchy, to say the least. So, just as Ignatius of Loyola had done, he went back to school, sitting alongside little boys to learn the rudiments of Latin grammar.

Though the Council of Trent had laid down rigid academic requirements for Church students, they were not yet being rigidly applied; otherwise, Camillus might never have become a priest. To the end of his days he insisted that he had never really learned any theology, and we have no reason to accuse him of false modesty.

As it was, the year 1583 saw him safely ordained by Thomas Goldwell, a bishop exiled from his Welsh diocese because he had refused to knuckle under to King Henry the Eighth.

Immediately afterwards Camillus went home for a visit, his first in many years. Once again we can imagine the surprise among the locals when the wild boy from the big house appeared among them as a priest.

Back in Rome, storms awaited him. Philip Neri did not approve of the new society—apparently he felt that Camillus was not the man to establish a new religious order. How comforting for us that even saints can sometimes be wrong!

More serious was the opposition of the hospital authorities. As we know, they had looked with a jaundiced eye on Camillus's prayer-meetings. Now they were horrified to discover that the members had bound themselves by vows.

There was a painful scene in the hospital courtyard when one of the governors, Msgr. Cusano, publicly accused Camillus of being a revolutionary—which, in a very real sense, he was. It is good to know that the Monsignor's attitude changed in time and he became one of Camillus's most influential supporters.

For the moment, however, Camillus was bewildered

and sad. Once again the Figure on the crucifix encouraged him—this time when he was wide awake. "Why distress yourself, man of little soul?" it said. "Go on with your enterprise, I will help you. Remember, this work is mine, not yours!"

Camillus and his colleagues moved to another hospital—Santo Spirito, on the banks of the Tiber. Here, conditions were even worse than at San Giacomo: of ten thousand patients admitted during a single year, more than nine thousand died. Yet it was here that the new society formed its character: here that Camillus drew up its first rules.

Normally, the brothers were to live, work, eat and pray together—but whatever happened, the sick must come first. Any rule might be suspended if their needs demanded it.

Camillus taught his men the art of nursing: how to help very weak patients to eat, holding their heads up and encouraging them; how to study each case and give a full report to the doctors; how to give bed-baths and how to move patients gently.

Not that he himself was always gentle: occasionally he was clumsy. Once he knocked the iron knob from a bed-canopy and the patient got a nasty head-wound. Camillus stayed with him all night, and in the morning the wound was healed.

There were other remarkable cures. A man about to undergo an amputation found his leg whole after Camillus had spent the night at his bedside; years later he embarrassed Camillus greatly by greeting him joyfully in the street and telling bystanders what had happened.

In March, 1586, the new order was formally approved by the Vatican and Camillus was elected its first Superior-General. Soon afterwards came a summons from the shrewd and dynamic Pope Sixtus the Fifth, who

wanted to see this remarkable apostle of the sick for himself. The Pope promised Camillus every assistance and
granted permission for the distinctive red cross to be
worn on the brothers' cassocks.

Soon that cross was known and loved throughout
Rome and throughout Italy. Men stopped to kiss it as its
wearers, ever-growing in number, hurried to the aid of
the sick even when others had fled in terror—as they did
during the frequent plague epidemics.

If a priest or a brother was stricken down—and many
were—another stepped in to take his place. Camillus saw
170 of his men die on duty, yet at the end of his life his
order was still 300 strong.

At first people called them "the Company of Camillus". Their founder did not care for this and so they
called themselves the Ministers of the Sick, which remains their official title to this day. Nevertheless, it is as
the Camillans that we in the English-speaking countries
know them best.

Over a door in one of his houses, Camillus wrote:
"Brother, if you do a bad thing with pleasure, the pleasure passes and the badness remains. If you wearily do a
good thing, the weariness passes and the good remains."

Those words he himself lived to the full. His foot got
worse with the years. The terrible wound spread up to
the knee so that much of his leg was eaten away. He also
suffered from a rupture, from kidney-stones and from
severe corns. Ignoring all his complaints, he toiled
ceaselessly alongside his brethren, allowing himself only
four or five hours sleep each night.

During the terrible August of 1590, when floods,
epidemic and famine struck Rome in rapid succession,
he organised food supplies as well as medical aid, trudg-
ing through the streets with two goats at his heels, giving
milk to starving babies.

When a cardinal detained him with polite inquiries, he exploded: "Your Eminence, I beg you for the love of God not to go on talking to me. I'm already late with this medicine!"

Camillus never really lost his fiery temper: he just learned to control it, and sometimes to use it. Bureaucrats who hampered relief work came off worse when they encountered him; and it always angered him to hear a patient spoken of with repugnance, no matter how nauseous the symptoms might be. Blasphemy, also, he could not bear. Once he came close to throwing an offender from the carriage in which they were fellow-passengers.

His flashes of anger were rare, however; he preferred cheerful firmness. One of his priests, unwilling to travel from Naples to Rome, protested that the doctor had ordered him not to go. "That is what the doctor has ordered—very well," replied Camillus briskly. "But obedience orders you a hat and a pair of spurs. Get ready to leave."

When two young English Protestants arrived in the order's Milan hospital, having injured each other in a fight, Camillus went in to see them. "My brothers," he demanded gravely, "how comes it that you, who are travelling companions and such good friends, have struck one another? And why don't you believe in God?"

He liked to repeat to his novices the advice which the Capuchin guardian had given him so many years before: "Whenever you have evil thoughts, spit in the devil's face." Now, all his aggression was reserved for Satan.

In 1607, Camillus resigned as General of the order and found himself, for the first time in many years, receiving orders rather than giving them. He did not find it easy. Reporting for work at the Rome hospital one morning, he asked the young priest in charge to assign him to a ward.

"Father, you must go wherever you please," replied the overawed priest.

"No, no," said Camillus. "You are the superior. You must direct me."

The young man indicated a ward, the easiest in the whole hospital. Camillus's jaw set, obedience forgotten.

"*You* can go there," he said firmly. "I'll go to this one." And off he marched to the ward where the work was grimmest.

At the end of his life he was afflicted by yet another ailment, which caused constant vomiting. He called his illnesses his "five blessings" and worked on until he knew that death was near.

Forced at last to go to bed, he sent a farewell letter to his brethren, telling them that their order was a miracle of God's grace "since it was founded by a sinner like myself, so ignorant and incompetent."

A procession of dignitaries flocked to his bedside— cardinals, ambassadors, heads of other religious orders, along with many humbler folk. When he had received the Last Sacraments he begged to be excused further visitors, since he wished to compose himself for death. A colleague interceded: those waiting had come far, wanting to increase their devotion.

"Their devotion?" Camillus snorted. "By seeing a man in bed with his body already half decayed? Let them go and practise charity in a hospital and not waste time looking at the worst of men!"

He asked for some Bologna sausage and ate it with real enjoyment. Shortly afterwards he died. The date: July 14th, 1614.

It is a curious coincidence that both the patrons of the sick, St. Camillus de Lellis and St. John of God, were ex-soldiers. St. Camillus is also, in his own right, the patron of all nurses.

Holiness for Busy
People

Shoulders hunched, the young man walked miserably along the street towards the Church of St. Etienne des Grés. From a doorway, a ragged beggar held out a filthy cap towards him "Alms, monsieur," he whined. As the youngster pressed a coin into it, he felt a stab of envy. The irony of his situation struck home to him but did not make him smile. That he, the son of a noble house, with money, brains and a brilliant career ahead of him, should envy this poor creature of the Paris gutter! And yet, the man would quite probably go to Heaven while he, Francis de Sales, had no hope of it.

In the church, kneeling before Our Lady's statue, he envied all of them: the peasants on his father's estate, the dullest of his fellow-students—even the condemned waiting for their fate in the jail. How much better off than himself they all were, with at least a chance of salvation!

"Lord," Francis prayed, "if I am not to be allowed to love you in Heaven, grant at least that I may love you as much as possible in this world, while I have the chance."

It took a few moments for the realisation to sink in—for him to understand what had happened to him. For suddenly, after months of despair, he felt peaceful. More than that, he felt happy—wildly so. Of course God loved him: what a fool he had been ever to doubt it! Christ had died for him, Francis, as he had died for all men. If he believed that, and loved God with all his heart, how could he fail to see Heaven?

What terrible sin, you may be wondering, had Francis committed that he had got into this state of spiritual despondency? The answer is, of course, none at all. He had simply fallen victim temporarily, to one of Satan's cruellest tricks—persuading us that we are losing when we are actually on top.

Francis was not the only saint to go through such a crisis; much the same thing happened to Ignatius Loyola in his cave at Manresa. But Ignatius was going through an intense and terrifying process of conversion—the transformation from great sinner to great saint.

Francis was a totally different character: urbane, gentle and witty: radiating good humor, wisdom and common-sense. To those who know only his writings he seems born to be a bishop, even born to be a saint, the Christian humanist *par excellence.* So it comes as something of a surprise to learn that he, too, once suffered the torment of scruples.

Francis was born, on August 21st 1567, in the ancient dukedom of Savoy, where France, Switzerland and Italy meet among the Alps. From the first he wanted to be a priest, but his father destined him for a secular career and after arts studies at the Jesuit College of Clermont in Paris, Francis obediently took a law degree at Padua.

He was all of twenty-six by the time he announced his true vocation; peppery old Monsieur de Boisy took it badly but Francis was determined. Through the influence of a cousin, he was appointed a canon of Geneva before being ordained priest on December 18th, 1593.

Geneva was not a happy diocese, for the city was the headquarters of Calvinism and the Catholic bishop,

Claude de Granier, dare not venture there. Instead he ruled as an exile from Annecy.

Apart from Geneva—which, for the moment at least, seemed a hopeless prospect—Bishop de Granier's biggest pastoral problem was the region known as the Chablais, along the South side of Lake Geneva. Here, the Calvinist heresy had made deep inroads, yet the bishop felt that it could be won back for the Church.

By this time Francis had made a deep impression on him and he was convinced that the young man's charm, intelligence and obvious holiness made him the one for the task. And so, despite fresh howls of protest from Monsieur de Boisy, Francis and his cousin were sent to the Chablais.

De Boisy might well fear for his son's safety, for the assignment was both difficult and dangerous. Bitter religious wars were fresh in everyone's mind, and there were plenty of Protestants around who were quite capable of knifing a priest on sight.

Assassination was only one of the dangers. Travelling through the countryside on a bitter winter night, Francis was attacked by a pack of wolves and only escaped by spending the night in a tree while the wolves bayed for his blood below. In the morning he was rescued by some kindly Calvinist peasants, who found him frozen and near to death. Thanks to their care he quickly revived, and soon Francis was eagerly talking to them about the faith which they had abandoned. In the end, they returned to it.

Thousands were converted by Francis's zealous ministry; by the time Bishop de Granier came on visitation, two-thirds of the Chablais was Catholic once more. There were even hints of miracles. Once, it was said, the dead child of a Protestant couple had revived when Francis prayed that it might at least live long enough to be baptised. . . .

His success reached the ears of Pope Clement VIII, who—though he had never met Francis—entrusted him with a difficult and highly secret mission. The young priest was to go into Geneva in lay disguise, seek out the leader of the Calvinists, Theodore Beza, and see whether there was any hope of bringing him back to the Church.

A madly impossible task, you may say. As well ask a young American priest to take a plane to Moscow and try to convert Mr. Kosygin. Perhaps so, but at this time Beza was close to eighty. Until he was twenty-nine—the same age as Francis—he had been a Catholic. Clement had heard rumors that, in these final years, his conscience was troubling him. In the light of what followed, the rumors could have been right.

At all events, Calvin's successor was completely disarmed by Francis's charm and learning, and thoroughly enjoyed their talks on grace, predestination and free-will. He never came back to the faith but he admitted to Francis, after an intense interior struggle, that a Christian could save his soul in the Catholic Church. Six years later, only a few days before his death, a woman in his household asked him what religion he ought to follow. The old man replied, in tears: "The faith of the Catholic Church is best".

When Bishop de Granier, who was also getting on in years, decided that he needed a coadjutor, it was a foregone conclusion that he would ask Pope Clement to appoint Francis and a foregone conclusion that Clement would say yes.

It was not, however, quite as simple as that. Eager to see this brilliant Francis de Sales for himself, Clement made him undergo an oral examination, conducted by the Sacred College of Cardinals. Chief among the examiners was St. Robert Bellarmine, the great Jesuit, who was so delighted with Francis's performance that he embraced him warmly.

No less delighted was Pope Clement, who willingly named Francis Co-adjutor Bishop of Geneva. A few months later Bishop de Granier died and Francis succeeded him.

Even had he never written any of those famous books or letters, Francis would be remembered and loved today—for his wisdom and urbanity, certainly; but most of all for his kindness and simplicity. His new post carried noble rank: he was known officially as the Prince and Bishop of Geneva. Yet when this prince went to visit his clergy—many of them desperately poor—he let it be known in advance that he wanted no special preparations. It was his wish to share the ordinary fare of the presbytery.

Despite this, one *curé* was ashamed because he could not afford a feast. His stammering apologies were genially cut short. "My friend," said Francis, "do you think I would have things any different? If you have bread, eggs, a little wine and water, then let us enjoy them!"

Like Philip Neri, he treated everyone, no matter how great or how humble, in exactly the same way. But where Philip used affectionate familiarity, Francis behaved with exquisite courtesy. If he met one of his servants on the street, he always raised his hat and addressed them with the polite *vous* rather than the familiar *tu*.

He frequently gave religious instruction to youngsters and these classes were often jolly affairs, punctuated by laughter as the bishop illustrated a serious point with a funny story. In preaching to adults, however, he was sparing with stories, funny or otherwise. He said that they should be used like mushrooms, solely to whet the appetite.

Francis wore himself out in the care of his large and difficult diocese. Sometimes he had to be firm, for Trent's reforms had not yet penetrated and he found himself with two rival chapters of canons, each jealous of its privileges. When one group, feeling itself slighted, threatened to boycott the Corpus Christi procession, Francis countered with a threat of excommunication!

Usually, however, it was his charm and gentleness that solved problems, above all in his work as a confessor and spiritual director.

Among the many souls whom he guided was another saint, Jane Frances de Chantal, with whom he founded the Order of the Visitation, which combined contemplative prayer with work for the poor. Jane was a widow who, while still young, lost her dearly-loved husband in a hunting accident. Before meeting Francis she had suffered a great many other trials, especially at the hands of an inept spiritual director. Under Francis's wise guidance, she found her true vocation—and found sainthood.

The most famous of his books, however, was written not for Jane but for another woman penitent, Madame de Charmoisy, a diplomat's wife who was actually related to Francis. From the day it was published in 1609 the *Introduction to the Devout Life* was a best-seller. Immediately recognised as a spiritual classic, it has scarcely ever been out of print and has been admired and used by thousands of non-Catholics, among them the great John Wesley.

It broke new ground by insisting—and demonstrating—that holiness could be achieved by ordinary people leading ordinary, busy lives; that everyday duties, trials—even amusements—all could be made stepping-stones to God. To us this is commonplace, simply because Francis has had such a tremendous influence. In his day it was so novel that some were shocked by it. One priest actually tore the book up in the pulpit, scandalised because Francis said that dancing, if properly conducted, was a lawful recreation.

Before Francis, the spiritual life had always implied some degree of alienation from everyday affairs. Philip Neri, it is true, gathered his disciples from people living in the world, but even he, as we saw, used methods that were deliberately eccentric. This would never have done for Francis, who said that people who wished to be religious should avoid ostentation, but should wear clothes that fit.

From his writings, and from his recorded remarks, it would be easy to cull a whole anthology of wit and wisdom. Here are just a few examples chosen at random:

> You can catch more flies with a spoonful of honey than with a hundred barrels of vinegar.

> Many people would be glad to have afflictions, so long as they were not inconvenienced by them.

> The crosses that we fashion for ourselves are always lighter than the ones laid on us.

> Do you want to walk earnestly towards devotion? Then get a good spiritual director to guide you; that is the best of all advice.

> Make yourself a seller when you are buying and a buyer when you are selling. That way you will sell and buy justly.

> Stay away from immoral people—especially if they are impudent, as they generally are.

> To become gentle, first be patient with your own faults.

It is practically impossible to pick up any book by him or about him, without being richly rewarded.

Francis died on December 28th, 1622, in a gardener's

cottage at Lyons, where he was lodged by the Visitation nuns whom he was visiting. Having suffered a rupture of a cerebral artery, he was subjected to the best treatment that medical science could offer, which involved burning his head with red-hot irons. Since he was bald, and since his scalp had already been blistered, the agony was all the greater. He bore it patiently, with scarcely a murmur, and breathed his last two hours later. He was canonised in 1665.

Revolution in the Classroom

As he trudged through the streets of Rheims towards the dying woman's bedside, Canon John Baptist de la Salle knew that this was no ordinary sick call. Madame de Croyère was not one of his penitents and he was not well acquainted with her. Nevertheless she had asked to see him.

John knew why and he was not looking forward to the visit.

When he entered the sick room the patient was still quite lucid, though his experience at deathbeds told him that she could not last much longer.

"My dear Canon, how very kind of you to come", she said graciously, extending a thin white hand.

"If I can be of any service, Madame," said John, as he took it in his own and bowed. He wished that he could have sounded more sincere.

If there was anything wrong in his manner, Madame de Croyère did not notice. She waved him to a chair, the nurse withdrew, and they proceeded to business.

Since she could not take her considerable fortune with her, she had decided to spend it on founding schools for the poor children who abounded in the historic French city. And she wanted John to undertake the work.

Of course it was a call from God, John told himself, as he walked slowly back through the dusk towards his house near the great cathedral. All the same, he wondered why it had come to him. For he had no special interest in education and—yes, he might as well admit it—he preferred to love the poor at a distance. His aristocratic background and his elegant classical education had set a wide gulf between himself and the ragged illiterates with whose schooling he was now charged.

He had, nevertheless, accepted the burden laid on him by the dying old lady. To refuse such a request would have been hard even for one less kind and courteous than John Baptist de la Salle. All the same, he wished that she had asked someone else. . . .

It was only by accident that Madame de Croyère had got hold of his name in the first place. A friend of his had died some time before and appointed John as his trustee. The friend had founded an orphanage for poor young girls, and one of John's duties had been to settle its affairs. So efficiently had he gone about this that, when Madame de Croyère conceived her plan, her own priest immediately recommended Canon de la Salle as the man to put it into effect.

At first it looked as though the whole operation might not be quite so painful as John had feared. An energetic layman, Monsieru Nyel, was engaged to conduct the day-to-day management of the schools, so that John did not have to become too deeply involved. Monsieru Nyel had come to Rheims from Rouen, where he had earned a considerable reputation as a school founder.

Monsieur Nyel was indeed good at founding—that became apparent very quickly. Full of enthusiasm, he swept from one district to another, setting up schools with great gusto. Unfortunately, though, he was not really interested in running them. His technique was to assemble a few desks, chairs and boys, put them in the charge of some rough young man who himself could hardly read or write, then rush on to the next foundation.

The chaos that followed can easily be imagined. In no time at all, a school would degenerate into riot. The poor young master, with no notion of keeping order, would lose all self-control and beat up as many of his charges as he could catch. Irate dads, themselves just as heavy-handed at home, would then march down to school to avenge the wrongs wreaked upon their tearful offspring—who, of course, had learned little or nothing in the meantime.

It was truly a desperate situation. Something had to be done—and fast. What John did caused a good deal of astonishment, especially to his friends, who knew him as a sensitive and fastidious man. Bidding farewell to the disastrous Monsieur Nyel, he took the uncouth young schoolmasters into his own house and proceeded to teach them their job.

Their ignorance appalled him and so did their table-manners. Nevertheless, he persevered. He was not a total stranger to the poor: as a church student in Paris he had visited hospitals and prisons, and later, as a priest, he had ministered to them at Rheims. All the same, he had never actually lived with them before and he did not find it easy.

In fact few of his first recruits stayed with him for long. But those who left were replaced by men of a different type—men who, though poor and uneducated, were none the less intelligent and devout. Men with a clear vocation to teaching. Men with, John soon began to realise, a vocation to the religious life.

In May, 1684, John took some of the group into retreat, at the end of which they took a vow of obedience. And so was born—almost, it seems, by accident—one of the Church's greatest teaching orders, the Brothers of the

Christian Schools. But of course, there was nothing accidental about it.

By now John had no doubt: it was God's will that he should devote himself completely to the education of poor boys, and to the order which he had founded. To the anger and derision of his family and many of his friends, he gave away his fortune, resigned his cathedral post, and became poor, like the young men who had thrown in their lot with him.

In vowing himself to poverty John was not simply giving up money, he was giving up a whole career—a career which might very possibly have been crowned with a bishop's mitre. In those days, clerical advancement was still governed very largely by family connections and class distinctions. Like Francis of Sales, John had actually been appointed a canon before he was ordained—in fact, at the ridiculously early age of fifteen. Once again, a well-placed cousin had secured the post for the young hopeful.

By adopting his new mode of life, he was turning his back on his whole background, and doing it right there in Rheims, where everyone could see. Small wonder, then, that family and friends were angry.

Like other clerics of his rank, John had always lived prosperously. In particular, he was used to eating well and he had a delicate appetite. Now, he deliberately got himself used to the coarsest possible food. Only after several days' fasting could he get it down.

His fasts became longer and more rigorous, and he began to spend whole nights in mental prayer. So severely did he flog himself with the discipline that the young brothers became frightened and tried to hide it. But John persisted in his penances, and so strict was the rule which he imposed on his men that people called them "little Trappists".

He got results, though; no one could deny that. Very

soon, the schools of Rheims and the surrounding towns were transformed. Instead of the old anarchy, peace and order reigned. The local clergy gaped as they saw ragged urchins transformed into happy and interested young-sters who worked enthusiastically at the three R's.

Not surprisingly, everyone wanted the brothers to come to *their* town. John was inundated with requests—far more than he could possibly cope with.

At the same time, he realised that many of the men who came to him, intelligent and devout though they were, either had no wish to become brothers, or sub-sequently turned out to have no vocation. Nevertheless, they had all the makings of excellent schoolmasters. Why waste all this potential, John asked himself. Why not train these young fellows and employ them as lay teachers?

In 1687, with forty freshmen, John set up a separate institution for just that purpose—the first training college for secular students in the whole history of education.

Where John had been derided, now he was sur-rounded by admirers. Some of these, people with money, asked to be associated permanently with his work; they offered to endow schools. There was an obvi-ous danger here—that the benefactors might want a say in management. John sought advice from Father Nicolas Barré, a saintly Franciscan who had been his friend from the beginning.

"Endow your schools and they will founder," said Nicolas bluntly. "Put yourself into the hands of Providence, and Providence will provide."

John took the advice, rejected all offers of endow-ments, and relied solely on God. He was not disap-pointed. Whenever money was needed, somehow it al-ways came.

Like Dominic and Ignatius, John had no wish to rule

over the order which he had founded, and he eventually succeeded in persuading its members to elect one of the wisest and most senior members, Brother Henry, to succeed him. John himself intended to perform the most menial tasks available.

This did not please the local archbishop, who apparently did not think it fitting that a priest—and a former canon at that—should find himself under obedience to a lay-brother. John met that objection by having Henry study for the priesthood, but unfortunately, Henry died before he could be ordained.

Rightly or wrongly, John took this as a sign of God's displeasure. Henceforth, he decreed, no brother should ever be ordained priest, nor would any priest be permitted to join the order. The rule holds to this day. Nothing, not even the priesthood, must distract the brothers from their work of study, teaching and prayer.

Another lasting rule John made at this time: there were to be no corporal penances. Brothers were not to use the discipline on themselves, for example, or to undertake any fasts other than those which the Church imposes on everyone. This is surprising in view of his own fierce asceticism, and it was in fact a reversal of his earlier policy. He had found that some of the younger men were damaging their health in their over-enthusiasm for bodily mortification—and good teachers needed to stay as fit as possible; so he put the brake on. Saints, too, learn by their mistakes!

In 1688 the order made its first move into Paris, to take over a poor school in the parish of St. Sulpice. In the capital, the work burgeoned just as it had done around Rheims. Soon the brothers were running a whole range of institutions: ragged schools, reform schools, schools for tradesmen's sons, Sunday schools for working lads. Well over a thousand youngsters were in their care.

When England's exiled monarch, James II, asked John to look after fifty youngsters from Ireland, John arranged special courses for them too.

As the work expanded, so the order expanded; recruits came flocking from all over France. And with them came other young men, sent by parish priests to be trained as teachers. For these John opened a second training-college in Paris.

He considered that teacher-training was probably the most important job the order had to do, because the need for teachers would always be greater than the order itself could ever hope to provide. "If I can't send out good teachers, then I'll send none at all," he declared; and ever since then the order has continued to concentrate especially on running these colleges. In the United States and all over the world, there are many fine teachers today who owe their training to the Brothers of the Christian Schools.

The order's success in Paris was neither miraculous nor surprising, for there, as elsewhere, the standard of education was abysmal. Only society's upper echelons could afford a decent education for their children; the rest had to rely largely on schools run by scholastic quacks. When the brothers came along, it was only natural that parents should make a beeline for them.

It was equally natural that the charlatan school proprietors, suddenly bereft of pupils, should react violently. Furious at the loss of fees, a group of these dignified gentlemen went down to one of the brothers' schools, forced their way in and wrecked the place (it was, fortunately, empty at the time).

At first John refused to take legal action against them, but under pressure from his friends, he eventually did so. He found himself with a powerful ally—Madame de Maintenon, the secret wife of Louis XIV. Despite her earlier, somewhat lurid reputation, Madame was a devout Catholic and an admirer of the new teaching brothers and their work. Yet not even her influence could check the hostility completely. The attacks on the schools continued.

Having failed to frighten the brothers out of Paris, the bully-boys next tried perjury and slander. John, they swore, was secretly on the make—taking fees from parents under the pretext of running charity schools. John challenged them to produce one parent from whom he had taken money. Of course they could not, but the case closed his schools down for three months.

So far, John's opponents had been the owners of the low-class private schools. But another group felt itself threatened by the new order—the writing-masters, who claimed an exclusive right to teach calligraphy. The two groups had previously been rivals. Now they joined forces against the brothers.

The writing-masters were a powerful corporation: they succeeded where the proprietors had failed. In 1704 they lodged an official complaint with the authorities, alleging that the brothers were encroaching on their prerogative and damaging their livelihood. Before anyone knew what was happening the police raided the schools and closed them. The brothers were fined fifty livres.

They refused to pay the fine and lodged an appeal. The authorities replied by charging them with contempt of court. The clergy, who had besieged John with requests for teachers, who had begged him to train their young men, made no move to help. Quietly, John and the brothers left town.

It was by far the most effective thing they could have done. As soon as the parents of their pupils realised what had happened, that the brothers had been driven out of Paris and were not coming back—what a storm broke! In the face of their mass opposition, authority caved in. The brothers returned to carry on with the good work.

Their troubles in the capital were far from over, however. For now the Church was split by the heresy of Jansenism, which gained an especially powerful hold in France.

The Jansenists—who took their name from a Dutch theologian—believed with St. Augustine that free will played little or no part in the work of salvation. Certain souls were saved, and others damned, simply because God had decided it that way from all eternity. In subtle forms, Jansenist influence has persisted almost down to our own time; in its day, this gloomy heresy corrupted a number of eminent churchmen—among them Archbishop Noailles of Paris.

Since John's views were orthodox, he soon found himself at loggerheads with the Archbishop, who set about depriving him of his position. Eventually he succeeded: John was made to stand down in favour of the Archbishop's nominee.

The brothers, loyal to John, revolted. They refused to accept the new man, although he asked them to do so, urging obedience to authority. He even withdrew to the South of France until, at the brothers' insistence, he came back and took over the reins once again.

He did manage to resign in the end; another wise and good brother was elected in his place and John spent his declining years in Rouen, working on the final version of the Rule and writing his great spiritual books, *Meditations* and *Method of Mental Prayer*. They are still used today, as is the text-book which he wrote during the early days of his work, *The Conduct of Schools*.

On Good Friday, April 9th, 1719, John Baptiste de la Salle died. His last words were appropriate indeed: "I adore in all things the providence of God towards me."

One-Way Ticket
to Rome

The crowd in St. Peter's Square were excited; now they were also bewildered. A few minutes before, the unmistakable white smoke had told them that a new Pope had been elected. Eagerly they pressed forward, waiting for the senior cardinal deacon to come out and tell them his name.

So far, however, there was no stately procession; no age-old Latin proclamation: "I announce to you a great joy. We have a Pope . . ."

Instead, from a window high in the Vatican Palace, a beaming official could be seen, waving a pair of scissors in the air and snipping happily away at an imaginary piece of cloth. Snip, snip, went the scissors. Snip, snip.

It only took a moment for the Italians to get the message. Of course! "It's Sarto!" they yelled gleefully. "Sarto is Pope!"

The scissors were a visual pun—the new Pope's surname, Sarto was the Italian word for "tailor". Almost before the cardinal deacon made his announcement, the news was humming along the wires. Giuseppe Sarto, Cardinal Patriarch of Venice, had become Pope Pius X.

"No need to pack so many things—I'm not going to America!" he had told his sisters, as he prepared to leave

Venice for the conclave. Convinced that he would be back within a fortnight, he bought a return railroad ticket. To friends who feared that he would not return, he declared: "Don't worry—I'll come back to Venice dead or alive!"

When he got five votes in the first ballot, he thought some of his colleagues in the Sacred College were playing a practical joke on him. Only when he tried to withdraw his name did he find that he was indeed a serious candidate. A group led by Cardinal Gibbons of Baltimore told him that it was his duty to let it remain.

He complied, still not expecting to be elected. As it became more and more obvious that he would be the final choice, he begged the cardinals not to go on voting for him. Pale and weeping, he insisted that he lacked the necessary qualities: they had a solemn duty to elect someone else.

His protests had no effect. On August 4th, 1903, fifty of the sixty-two cardinals voted for Giuseppe. Even then he tried to refuse. "Go back to Venice if you wish—but if you do, your conscience will hurt you for the rest of your life!" Cardinal Ferrari of Milan told him sternly. But the clinching argument came from another cardinal, who asked quite simply: "Do you wish to resist the Will of God?"

So Giuseppe Sarto—"Beppi" to his family and friends—ascended the Throne of Peter. For the first time since the Middle Ages, the Catholic Church had a peasant for its Pope.

That he had no intention of changing his simple ways, he made clear right from the outset. As he waited, newly dressed in his white robes, to give his first blessing to the world, the papal master of ceremonies suddenly pointed in horror at the gilt cross hanging round his neck.

"Your cross, Holy Father—it's tin!" declared the

shocked prelate. It was, too. Somebody had once given Cardinal Sarto a gold cross, but he had long ago pawned it and given the money to the poor. "Don't worry Monsignore," the new Pope reassured him with a wan smile. "At this distance, nobody will notice what it's made of." And nobody did.

When he retired to his room at the end of that first, hectic day, Pope Pius realised with alarm that a young Swiss Guard was preparing to stand sentry there all night. "My dear fellow, go to bed and then we can both get some rest," he told him. "Don't worry—nobody will come to steal the Pope!"

But the Pope did not get any rest, either that night or for four nights afterwards, as he confided to a friend later on. During those long, sleepless hours in the papal apartment he must often have looked back over the long journey that had brought him there.

When he first became a cardinal, and people started calling him "Your Eminence", he used sometimes to reply, with amused irritation: "I'm the son of a poor family of Riese. What's so eminent about that?"

And indeed, his start in life could scarcely have been humbler. Born on June 2, 1835, he was the second and eldest surviving son of Riese's parish clerk— a job which included that of postmaster. His mother, Margherita, was a dressmaker, much younger than her husband.

A year before the future Pope was born there had been another son, also called Giuseppe, but he did not survive. Altogether there were ten children and life was a constant struggle. When little "Beppi" Sarto won a scholarship, at the age of ten, to the high school at Castelfranco, he used to walk there and back barefoot—a round trip of ten miles—carrying his lunch, a piece of bread, in his pocket.

The whole area where they lived, in the province of

Venetia, was then under Austrian rule, and so young Giuseppe grew up amid the political tensions which he would later have to deal with as Pope. Though he was always a devout youngster, he certainly had his faults— among them a temper which sometimes got him into fights.

Giuseppe was a seminary student of seventeen when his father died, only a few days after the birth of his youngest child. It was a terrible blow, but Margherita Sarto would not hear of her son giving up his vocation to support the family. "We will manage somehow," she said. And manage they did.

Since Giuseppe's brilliance and hard work had got him through the seminary course eight months ahead of time, by special permission he was ordained priest before his twenty-third birthday. His first appointment was a curate in the village of Tombolo, where he rapidly built up a reputation for the eloquence of his preaching and the shabbiness of his clothes. Any money he got was immediately given to the poor, and for years he refused to buy himself a new coat even though his old one was practically threadbare.

He distressed the housekeeper greatly by eating next to nothing and sleeping for only four hours a night. "He's as thin as a breadcrust!" she complained. His ability to live on very little sleep constantly amazed people, but it stood him in good stead when he became Pope. His capacity for work was enormous.

As a parish priest in the farming town of Salzano he now had his sisters to keep house for him. He continued to drive them to despair by his refusal to spend anything on himself. When he did get an overcoat, he gave it away to a poor man one winter day.

But with all his goodness, he had a puckish sense of humor, and sometimes he turned it to good advantage.

When a man whom he knew to be a very indifferent Catholic asked him one day for a job reference, Giuseppe told him to call by the presbytery on Friday afternoon to collect it.

At lunchtime on Friday, he walked up to the man's home and—as he had expected—detected a strong odor of frying meat. Later in the day, the man called for his reference. Opening the door to him, Giuseppe assumed an air of wide-eyed surprise.

"There must be some mistake," he said. "Today can't be Friday—you had meat for lunch!"

The sexton at Salzano was elderly and found it hard to get up in the mornings. Consequently, he was sometimes late in opening up the church and ringing the bell for Mass.

An officious parishioner, arriving early at church one morning, was horrified to see the parish priest himself swinging hard on the bell-rope.

"Don Sarto, that is no job for a man in your position," he exclaimed. "Just wait a moment and I'll go and waken up that lazy sexton!"

"Please do nothing of the kind," replied Giuseppe cheerfully. "He is old, I'm young and fit. Do you think it is any trouble to me to ring the bell?"

One of his best friends in Salzano was a Jewish mill-owner who often used to give him money when he wanted to help somebody in trouble. Beppi, for his part, would help the industrialist with labor and welfare problems in the factory. As it happened he also had Jewish friends in Tombolo, where, during his days as a curate, he used to earn a little extra by acting as tutor to their children.

But whatever money he got, it never stayed in his pocket for long. "He says yes to everyone," moaned his sister, Rosa, "and he's all skin and bone". Like the rest of the family, she worried constantly about his thinness, but thin or not, Giuseppe continued to work almost the clock round.

Truly his energy seemed limitless. In 1873, during a terrible cholera epidemic, he slaved tirelessly among the sick, totally unafraid of catching the disease himself. Wherever anyone was afraid or dying, there was Giuseppe with a word of cheer. People felt better just through looking at him.

When the local hospital badly needed repairs, Giuseppe plunged into debt to pay for the work. The thought that he might be running the parish into bankruptcy never seemed to occur to him, so total was his confidence in God. And of course, God never let him down.

When a fierce fire broke out in a hayrick, the terrified screams brought Giuseppe running to the scene. The flames were licking out towards the adjacent farmhouse, and the family seemed certain to lose their home.

"Don't worry," said Giuseppe calmly, "the house won't be touched."

The moment he had spoken, the wind suddenly veered and carried the flames harmlessly in the opposite direction. Only the hay was lost.

Soon afterwards, a blight hit the tobacco crop, causing the leaves to curl and die. Scores of small farmers faced ruin. Giuseppe rang the church bell to summon everyone, then told them to kneel and pray for deliverance from the blight. It disappeared immediately and the crop was saved.

It was not surprising that people began to call Giuseppe, not Don Sarto but Don *Santo*—the saint.

But this saint, like many another, had a sound business head. Realising that the poor farmers were putting their whole lives in pawn to rapacious moneylenders, he got together a few wealthy friends and with their help formed a credit fund which lent cash at a low rate of interest—just enough to keep the fund going. It was a huge success, but now his happy days at Salzano were numbered.

During his curacy at Tombolo, the bishop had offered him a teaching post in the seminary, but he had asked to remain where he was. "I'm just a simple country priest and I always will be," he explained. Now, once again, the bishop asked him to move to the seminary, this time to take charge of the students' spiritual formation. Just as before, Giuseppe tried to decline, and for the same reason. But this time, the bishop would not take no for an answer.

So Giuseppe moved, with a sad heart, to Treviso. There he stayed for nine years, looking after the students and also acting as the chancellor of the diocese, handling much of the administrative work.

One day a student came to him in deep distress: his parents were facing ruin for want of 150 lire. Ruefully, Giuseppe pulled out the little money he had in his pocket, only a fraction of the required sum.

"But don't worry—I'll get it for you," he said. Sure enough, the money was there on the following day. Giuseppe, as usual, had borrowed it from someone he knew would gladly wait for repayment.

Everyone realised it but Giuseppe himself—it was only a matter of time before he would be appointed a bishop. Once, during a business visit to Tunisia, the Archbishop of Carthage had sheltered him with his cape when they were caught in a shower of rain. "The purple suits you," said the archbishop, "and the pope who clothes you in it will be greatly honored."

Giuseppe brushed the prophecy aside with a joke— but he did not laugh when, not long afterwards, his own bishop summoned him to the chapel and, after they had said a prayer together, handed him a letter informing him that he was to be Bishop of Mantua.

Giuseppe tried to evade the promotion just as, later on, he tried to flee from the papacy. He wrote a long letter to Rome, setting out all the reasons why he should not be appointed. Back came the reply, one word, written in his own hand by Pope Leo XIII. "Obey!"

So Giuseppe obeyed, and was consecrated bishop. Soon afterwards, he went home to Riese and showed his mother the episcopal ring which he had been given. Signora Sarto held out her own work-worn hand, with the simple gold wedding-band on the third finger. "You have a beautiful ring, Beppi," she said, "but you would not be wearing it today if I had not first worn this one."

In Rome, Leo XIII soon had cause to be proud that he had chosen Giuseppe for Mantua. "He is the best bishop in Lombardy!" he told his aides.

He was, too. The biggest problem facing the diocese was a shortage of priests: during Giuseppe's first year only one was ordained, though forty were needed. So the new bishop launched a campaign for vocations, one of the most energetic the Church has ever seen.

He took over personally the running of the seminary, engaged the best professors and taught some of the more important courses himself. He told his priests to keep a constant look-out for young men who might possibly be called to the priesthood and ordered that they be given every encouragement and brought to see him at the earliest opportunity.

Many a youngster, looking into that wise and saintly face, realised for certain where his future lay. Within a very few years, nearly 150 new priests had been ordained.

Like Francis de Sales, he told his priests that he wanted no special preparations when he called: the ordinary fare of the presbytery was good enough for him. He kept in constant touch, knew all their problems—and had his own way of dealing with those who were not up to scratch.

One parish priest had got especially careless in his duties: he was constantly late in getting to church so that people who wanted to go to confession before Mass had no opportunity to do so. When the laggard arrived one morning, late as usual, he was astonished to find that someone was already hearing confessions.

Pulling back the curtain, he found himself face to face with Bishop Sarto. Crestfallen, he waited for the rebuke. It did not come.

"Any time you have trouble getting to church, Father, just let me know," said Giuseppe gently. "I'll always be happy to stand in for you." That priest was never late again.

Giuseppe really did love everybody, including the enemies of the Church. Of these there were plenty, in an Italy ruled largely by anticlericals. One day, a certain citizen of Mantua penned a newspaper article libelling its bishop, an offence for which he could have been sent to jail.

Despite the advice of his assistants, Giuseppe refused to prosecute, or to take any other action. "What that poor man needs is prayer, not punishment," he declared.

When, soon afterwards, the libeller went bankrupt and it looked as though he really would go to jail, it was Giuseppe who saved him by sending him money anonymously. "Say that it is a gift from Our Lady of Perpetual Help," he told the messenger.

When, in the year 1893, Leo XIII announced that Bishop Giuseppe Sarto was to be a cardinal and also Patriarch of Venice, Giuseppe once more begged to be excused. Predictably, he request was denied.

Living as we do, in a world hungry for success, we

might be tempted to suspect something phoney in this constant reluctance to accept honors. We have to remember that saints do not see things as we do, for they measure themselves against perfection—the perfection that each of us might achieve if we loved God according to the fullest measure of our opportunity. They are more truly conscious of their own small imperfections than we are of our great ones. Giuseppe genuinely feared that if he took on too much responsibility for the souls of others, he might fail in the end and so lose his own.

In those days of strained relations between church and state, no Catholic bishop could take up his post without first obtaining the permission of the local authority, and it took the city government of Venice fifteen months to approve Cardinal Sarto's nomination.

When they finally got round to giving him their secular blessing, the overjoyed Catholics of the city prepared a mighty welcome. A thousand gondolas were to accompany him, he was told, as he sailed in the King's barge up the Grand Canal.

What Giuseppe thought of that you can probably imagine. "Couldn't I just arrive quietly, shut up in a big crate?" he asked plaintively.

When the great day came, however, he endured it well enough, consoling himself with the thought that all these cheers, flags and bunting were really for Jesus, not for poor Giuseppe Sarto from Riese.

Cardinal Patriarch of Venice—it is certainly a title to roll round the tongue, a title which somehow conjures up all the pomp and splendor of the Renaissance. Yet this Cardinal Patriarch wore the purple trappings of his office as little as possible. Instead he wandered, in a plain black cassock, up and down the alley-ways and canals, chatting to the gondoliers and the fishermen, sharing his tobacco with them, handing out candy to the children.

He was still the despair of his sisters, giving away money as fast as he got it, so that sometimes he had to borrow to pay the household bills. When someone gave him a beautiful clock, he lamented the fact that it bore his episcopal coat of arms. "I'll never be able to hock that," he said with a grin.

That he could be both tough and astute, the anticlericals who ran Venice swiftly discovered to their cost. With the terse slogan "Work! Pray! Elect!" he urged the Catholics to throw the enemies of the Church out of office. Two years later, that is exactly what they did.

Now that there was a Christian majority on the city council, Giuseppe's hand was greatly strengthened as he set out to attack poverty and injustice. With a fervor that would have done credit to any socialist, he presided at workers' meetings and berated employers who kept their labor force on starvation pay while they themselves soaked up big profits. He brought the lace industry back to Venice, and provided jobs for thousands. . . .

Now the simple country priest was pastor of the whole Church. It was during those first sleepless nights, surely, that he composed his first letter to his worldwide flock—a letter in which he announced his intention to "restore all things in Christ".

Having seen so many drastic changes in our own day, we may find it difficult to appreciate just how revolutionary was the reign of Pius X not so long before.

His first action was a strong one—to make sure that never again would the Church allow any nation to intervene in a papal election. This was prompted by a dramatic incident during the conclave that had just elected him.

At one point it seemed as though the Sicilian Cardinal Rampolla, a distinguished Vatican diplomat who had served as Secretary of State, would be chosen. As soon as the possibility became real, a Polish cardinal, who had been given prior instructions by the Austrian Emperor, made it clear that Austria would veto Cardinal Rampolla if he were in fact elected. They objected to him because they thought him pro-French. The other cardinals—Giuseppe Sarto among them—were outraged and indignant, but Cardinal Rampolla resolved the impasse by making a dignified withdrawal.

Today, thanks to Pius X, any such outside interference would be unthinkable.

Next he turned to Church government. It was, he knew, tangled and inefficient, with congregations overlapping one another in their areas of responsibility. The Pope had it streamlined. Church law, too, he ordered to be codified so that it was readily available and no longer scattered through many different volumes.

Music had always been very dear to his heart: as a youngster in the seminary he had fallen in love with Gregorian chant, the ancient liturgical song of the Church. Unfortunately, it was then not much heard outside colleges and monasteries; fashionable churches in London, Rome and Paris were much more likely to hire opera-singers to warble arias during Mass. Pius X banished the opera-singers and decreed that Gregorian chant be promoted as widely as possible.

All these were important changes, but they are quite overshadowed by another and greater change—one which affected the life of every practising Catholic. Above all, Pius X will be remembered as the Pope who encouraged frequent holy communion—it was, he insisted, a daily food and not a rare treat—and who made it possible for children to receive Our Lord at an early age.

Along with nearly all youngsters of that time, Giuseppe Sarto had to wait until he was eleven to make his own first communion, and he often complained at the delay.

"Don't worry, Beppi," the parish priest used to tell him jovially, "when you're the Pope you can change the rules."

Well, now Beppi *was* the Pope, and change the rules he did. He decreed that children should receive when they understood what they were doing—usually at about seven. Not that there was anything sacrosanct about a seventh birthday, as the Pope himself demonstrated when he received an English lady and her little boy in audience.

"How old are you, sonny?" asked the Pope.

"Four," the child replied.

"And can you tell me who it is people receive when they go to holy communion?"

"Yes, Jesus."

"And who is Jesus?"

"He's God," the boy replied promptly.

"Excellent!" said the Pope. Turning to his mother, he told her: "Bring him to Mass in my private chapel tomorrow morning. I will give him holy communion myself."

Among the thousands of clerical students in Rome when Pius X's reign began was a young man named Angelo Giuseppe Roncalli. Though nobody knew it then, he, too, was destined to become Patriarch of Venice and then Pope. We know him better as John XXIII, the pontiff who threw open the windows of the Church and let in the fresh air. But it was Pius X who unfastened the window and clearly inspired the youngster who was one day to be his successor.

In small things and great, the two men resembled one another amazingly. When they were elected, each wept because he would never see Venice again. Both hated Vatican stuffiness and formality—and in particular, being carried along in the *sedia gestatoria,* the portable papal throne. Pope John complained that it made him feel seasick; Pius X, too, used to feel queasy whenever he was hoisted aloft in it.

It was Pius who first broke the centuries-old rule that popes eat alone: when he announced that he proposed to have guests to lunch, his shocked aides told him that this had not been done since the days of Pope Urban VIII.

"Very good. Urban VIII was Pope, so he had the right to make the rule," Pius replied. "Now I'm Pope and I have the right to unmake it."

He put a firm stop to the custom of kissing the Pope's foot. "Don't do that, my dear friend," he told one cardinal who attempted it, "I'm so afraid I might kick you in the nose!"

Just as he had done when he first became a parish priest, he had his sisters move in to look after him. By now they had given up as a lost cause their attempt to stop him from giving every lira away. "I'm sorry that I can't send you any more than this," the Pope wrote to one needy priest, "but I myself am a beggar." And indeed, he depended constantly on the generosity of others.

Long before he was dead, those who lived close to the Pope knew that they were in the presence of a saint. Soon, others knew it too.

At a general audience, a man with a paralysed arm suddenly begged the Pope to cure him. "Yes, yes, yes," said the Pope, gently stroking the arm. Then he turned away quickly.

"Holy Father, Holy Father!" the man cried out excitedly. The Pope, knowing what he would reveal, turned back and pleaded, with a swift sign, that he remain silent. But cures like that could not stay secret for long—and there were many more.

A paralysed German boy, whose legs had never moved, was brought to an audience by his parents. The Pope came over and lifted the little boy gently.

"Come on, son," he said. "Let me see you try to walk."
At once, the child turned and ran back to his parents.

Two nuns, both dying of cancer, were granted a private
audience. When they emerged from his study their
friends, waiting in an ante-room, reeled back with shock.
Both had gone in looking desperately ill and weak. Now
they were glowing with health.

Outside in St. Peter's Square, the cab-driver would not
believe that these were the nuns whom he had brought
and refused to accept the fare.

Sometimes he did not have to be present to effect a
cure: his blessing, telegraphed over long distances, was
enough. The mother superior of an orphanage in India,
apparently dying, was healed in this way.

"They say I am working miracles, as though I had nothing else to do," the Pope joked, trying to laugh off the
reports that by now were circulating far beyond Rome.

When he finally had to admit what was happening, he
insisted: "It is not through any merit of my own. It is
through the power of the Keys that God grants these
favors". But if that were true, people asked, why did not
every Pope do the same?

At his election, Giuseppe Sarto had told his fellow-
cardinals: "I accept the papacy, but as a cross. And all of
you must help me to bear it."

In the eleven-year reign there were many crosses—one
of the worst of them being the heresy known as
Modernism, which swept through the Church at the beginning of the century. Despite its name, there was nothing particularly modern about it.

Religious dogma, said its proponents, was well and
good so long as nobody believed it too literally. Man's
religious sentiment was a valid part of his nature, but it
took different forms in every age, and Catholic dogma
was merely the particular expression of it that happened
to suit our own. So the Resurrection, for example need

not be accepted as an historical event; it was simply a myth which expressed man's unconquerable spirit and his refusal to despair in the face of death.

Perhaps a saint was needed to cope with an attitude that was at once so enticing and so deadly, preserving the outward form and sentiment of religion while cutting out its heart. At any rate, Pius X did deal with it, firmly and decisively; most modernists heeded his warnings and abjured their errors, but others did not and some fine minds were thereby lost to the Church.

Some of them—the Biblical scholar Alfred Loisy for example—were French, and France caused the Pope much heartache for other reasons.

In 1905 the anticlerical government repudiated the concordat made with Napoleon and decreed that Church and State must be separate. It wanted lay bodies known as *associations cultuelles* to take over Church property, but since its members would not even need to be practising Catholics, Pope Pius refused to accept them.

Some French Catholics wanted him to do a deal with the French Government in case the Church lost its property altogether. Of them, the Pope remarked: "They are thinking too much of material goods, not enough of spiritual." And soon he was proved right, because, although the Church did suffer materially, she was at least now free to appoint bishops without seeking Government approval—something that she had been compelled to do under the concordat.

In Italy, relations were happier. The Pope was able to ease somewhat the tensions between Church and State, and he made it possible for Catholics once more to vote in parliamentary elections.

Soon, however, a great sadness began to take hold of his mind, a sadness that outweighed all his other worries and problems. Again and again he spoke to his aides of "the great war which is coming". He even foretold the time of its outbreak, the summer of 1914, although 1914 was still some years away and few could see any particular likelihood of world conflict.

When war broke out first in Libya, then in the Balkans, his aides thought that this was what he had predicted, but he shook his head. "This is nothing, compared with what will come," he said.

On June 28th, 1914, the Austrian Archduke Ferdinand and his wife were assassinated and the powder-keg was lit. The Pope begged the Austrian Emperor to stay his hand, but the letter was never delivered.

"If I cannot protect so many young lives, who can, who will?" he asked, in anguish. And he added: "This is the last affliction that the Lord will visit on me. I would gladly give my life to save my poor children."

Eleven years before, the first pilgrims the new Pope had received were a group from the United States. "I love these Americans," he declared then, "they are the youth of Catholicism in bloom." And he sent his blessing to the whole nation.

By a coincidence, the last pilgrim group to see Pope Pius X were also Americans. On August 20, 1914, as the armies of Europe faced each other, he died of a broken heart.

"I will come back to Venice dead or alive," he had promised. He kept his word. Before he was finally buried in St. Peter's, his body was carried solemnly in a black-draped gondola along the Grand Canal.

A few days later, his will was read. It said: "I was born poor, I have lived poor, and I wish to die poor." That wish, at least, was fulfilled.

His canonisation, on May 29, 1954, was conducted by Pope Pius XII, who had worked in the Vatican throughout his reign and knew personally the man whom he now proclaimed a saint.

BIBLIOGRAPHY

Butler's Lives of the Saints (4 vols.) ed. H. Thurston SJ and D. Attwater. Burns Oates, London, 1956.

The Saints, A Concise Biographical Dictionary. ed. John Coulson. Hawthorn Books, New York, 1958.

The Popes, A Biographical History. ed. Eric John. Burns Oates, London, 1964.

Warriors of God, by Walter Nigg. Secker and Warburg, London, 1959. Fifty Great Modern Lives, by H. and D.L. Thomas. Hanover House, Garden City, NY, 1946.

The Journeys of St. Paul, by Stewart Perowne. Hamlyn Books, London, 1973.

Paul, Apostle Extraordinary, by M. Muggeridge and A.L. Vidler. Collins, London, 1972.

The Life of St. Anthony, by St. Athansius. tr. R.T. Meyer. Newman Press, Westminster, Md., 1950.

The Desert Fathers. tr. Helen Waddell. Fontana Books, London, 1965.

Six Saints for Parents, by R. Haughton. Burns Oates, London, 1962.

Confessions of St. Augustine. tr. F.J. Sheed. Sheed and Ward, London, 1944.

Early Church Portrait Gallery, by Maisie Ward. Sheed and Ward, London, 1959.

Saints and Sinners of the Fourth Century, by Marjorie Strachey. Kimber, London, 1958.

St. Brigid of Ireland, by Alice Curtayne. Browne and Nolan, Dublin, 1955.

St. Brigid, by D.P. Mould. Clonmore and Reynolds, Dublin, 1964.

St. Gregory the Great, by P. Battifol. tr. J.L. Stoddard. Burns Oates, London, 1929.

St. Benedict, by L. von Matt and S. Hilpisch. tr E. Graf OSB. Burns Oates, London, 1961.

The Holy Rule, by H. van Zeller OSB. Sheed and Ward, London, 1958.

Anglo-Saxon Saints and Scholars, by E.S. Duckett. Macmillan, New York, 1947.

Saga of Saints, by Sigrid Undset. Sheed and Ward, London, 1934.

St. Bernard of Clairvaux, by his contemporaries. tr. G. Webb and A. Walker. Mowbray, London, 1960.

St. Bernard of Clairvaux, by G. Cattaui. tr. E. Dargan. Clonmore and Reynolds, Dublin, 1966.

St. Dominic, by L. von Matt and M-H. Vicaire. Longman's, London, 1957.

Life of St. Dominic, by B. Jarrett, OP. Blackfriars Pubs., London, 1955.

St. Dominic, by Sr. Mary Jean Dorcy, OP. Herder, St. Louis, 1959.

St. Thomas Aquinas, the Angelic Doctor, by W. Norman Pittenger. Franklin Watts, New York, 1967.

St. Thomas Aquinas, Angel of the Schools, by J. Maritain. Sheed and Ward, London, 1933.

St. Catherine of Siena, by C.M. Antony. Burns Oates, London, 1915.

Three Ways of Love, by Frances Parkinson Keyes. Peter Davies, London, 1964.

The Life of St. Teresa of Avila, by herself. tr. D. Lewis. Burns Oates, London, 1962.

The Eagle and the Dove, by V. Sackville-West. Michael Joseph, London, 1943.

The Apostle of Rome, by Meriol Trevor. Constable, London, 1966.

St. Ignatius Loyola: The Pilgrim Years, by James Brodrick, SJ. Burns Oates, London, 1956.

The Spiritual Exercises of St. Ignatius. Burns Oates, London, 1952.

Francois de Sales, by M. de la Bedoyere. Collins, London, 1960.

The Gentleman Saint, by Margaret Trouncer. Hutchinson, London, 1963.

Introduction to the Devout Life, by St. Francis de Sales. tr M. Day, Cong. Orat. Burns Oates, London, 1956.

Life of St. Camillus, by C.C. Martindale, SJ. Sheed and Ward, London, 1946.

St. John Baptist de la Salle, by W.J. Battersby. Burns Oates, London, 1957.

The Great Mantle, by K. Burton. Clonmore and Reynolds, Dublin, 1951.

St. Pius X, by Walter Diethelm OSB. Vision Books, New York, 1956.